# NAIS

*Journal of the* NATIVE AMERICAN *and*
INDIGENOUS STUDIES ASSOCIATION

## VOLUME 10.1

Spring 2023

T0338065

*NAIS* (ISSN 2332-1261) is published two times a year in spring and fall (Northern Hemisphere) by the University of Minnesota Press, 111 Third Avenue South, Suite 290, Minneapolis, MN 55401-2520. http://www.upress.umn.edu

Postmaster: Send address changes to *NAIS,* University of Minnesota Press, 111 Third Avenue South, Suite 290, Minneapolis, MN 55401-2520.

Information about manuscript submissions can be found at naisa.org, or inquiries can be sent to journal@naisa.org.

Books for review should be addressed to *NAIS* Journal, The University of Texas at Austin, 150 W. 21st Street, Stop B3700, Austin, TX 78712-1155.

Address subscription orders, changes of address, and business correspondence (including requests for permission and advertising orders) to *NAIS,* University of Minnesota Press, 111 Third Avenue South, Suite 290, Minneapolis, MN 55401-2520.

## SUBSCRIPTIONS

- Individual subscriptions to *NAIS* are a benefit of membership in the Native American and Indigenous Studies Association. NAISA's tiered membership ranges from $25 to $100 annually. To become a member, visit http://naisa.org/.
- For current institutional subscriptions and back issue prices, please visit http://www.upress.umn.edu/.
- Digital subscriptions to *NAIS* for institutions are now available online through the Project MUSE Journal Collections Program at https://muse.jhu.edu/.

# NAIS

*Journal of the* NATIVE AMERICAN *and*
INDIGENOUS STUDIES ASSOCIATION

# CONTENTS

**VOLUME 10 ● ISSUE 1**

*Spring 2023*

## Articles

## Notes From the Field

## Reviews

SARA ČERNE

# "It Carries My Feet to These Places":
# The Mississippi in Joy Harjo's
# and Heid E. Erdrich's Poetic Remappings

## Abstract

Memory, place, and Indigenous resistance are explored in two poems whose central metaphor is the Mississippi River and the landscape near its delta and its source, respectively: "New Orleans" (1983) by the former U.S. Poet Laureate Joy Harjo (Muscogee) and "Pre-Occupied" (2013) by the Minneapolis-based Heid E. Erdrich (Turtle Mountain Ojibwe) in its textual and collaborative video poem versions. I analyze these poems' retheorizing of place by drawing on gender and Indigenous studies scholar Mishuana Goeman's concept of "remapping," arguing that the poems create an Indigenous Mississippi that replaces representations of the river as an icon of the U.S. empire and westward expansion. Both poets transcend regional and temporal boundaries, following the flow of the river to provide a broader definition of Indigenous homelands. Read together, "New Orleans" and "Pre-Occupied" traverse the three decades between their publication dates and the many miles that separate the Lower and the Upper Mississippi, demonstrating a riverine poetics that mimics the river's flow to enact a relational cartography that defies colonial mapmaking. The poems rhetorically reclaim the historically significant Indigenous space of the Mississippi River Valley and embody on the page a space in which land and cultural memory can come together. In their remappings, both poets turn away from settler cities and their monuments toward rivers, presenting them as repositories of Native memories and suggesting that the health and future of Indigenous stories and waterways are closely linked.

IN 2017, VISUAL ARTIST ANDREA CARLSON (Grand Portage Ojibwe) projected an image of Spirit Island, a sacred Dakota site that the Army Corps of Engineers had destroyed about half a century earlier, onto a Mississippi River lock and dam in downtown Minneapolis. The words "Dakhóta Makhóčhe," Dakota Land, appeared in bold white letters over orange lighting, first in Dakota, then in

Anishinaabemowin and English. Since the late nineteenth century, the physical island had been diminishing as settlers extracted it for limestone, using it to construct buildings in the Twin Cities and beyond. Spirit Island vanished in 1963 as the U.S. Corps of Engineers removed it to make room for boat traffic bound for the Upper St. Anthony Falls Lock and Dam. Carlson's installation, *Uncompromising Hand*, responds to the destruction of Indigenous sacred sites in the name of urban development or archeological knowledge production, bringing a physically erased past into the present by relocating it in place. Explaining that not including the island on the map was "the first step in imagining its absence," Carlson then demonstrates that Indigenous creation counters colonial erasure inherent in conventional mapping.[1]

Carlson's work visualizes and makes concrete the remapping and artistic reclaiming of the space of the Mississippi that takes place in the Indigenous poetry at the heart of this essay. I explore memory, place, and Indigenous resistance in two poems whose central metaphor is the Mississippi River and the landscape near its delta and its source, respectively: "New Orleans" (1983) by the 2019–2022 U.S. Poet Laureate Joy Harjo (Muscogee) and "Pre-Occupied" (2013) by the Minneapolis-based Heid E. Erdrich (Turtle Mountain Ojibwe) in its textual and collaborative video poem versions.[2] I analyze these poems' retheorizing of place by drawing on gender and Indigenous studies scholar Mishuana Goeman's concept of "remapping."[3] Harjo's and Erdrich's poems remap the Mississippi by reinscribing Indigenous stories and memory onto settler representations of the river. Opposing the widespread omission of Indigenous influences from accounts of the Mississippi and the confinement of Native people to the distant past, the poems work hand in hand with literary scholar Jodi Byrd's critique of the all-too-frequent theorization of Indigenous People as "past tense presences" who remain only "spectral, implied and felt."[4]

Even the name "Mississippi," derived from the Ojibwe "Misi-ziibi" (big river), signals the long-standing relationship of Indigenous cultures from the Midwest and the Southeast to the river. From roughly the year 800 to about 1600, the Mississippi gave rise to prominent Native American cultures whose earthworks can still be seen all over the Mississippi River Valley from Winterville in Mississippi to Cahokia in Illinois to Aztalan in Wisconsin. Historically, the importance of the river can hardly be overstated, as it both sustained Indigenous tribes with its rich resources and connected them via its many tributaries. As archeologist Timothy Pauketat explains in his study of Cahokia, the Mississippi shaped landforms as well as peoples, acting as "a major transportation corridor, a political boundary, a rich resource zone, and a living symbol of the Mississippian cosmos."[5] The same river, however, played a major role in establishing settler geography. By the nineteenth century, the Mississippi came to demarcate the line between settler-occupied space and designated Indigenous territory on the map, acting as a boundary between two parts of the U.S. empire, as well as facilitating violent acts of Native removal.

Conventional mapping, explains Goeman in her Native feminist approach, is a patriarchal form of settler geography that erases Native people from historical memory and marks communal land as private property. As legal scholar Robert Miller demonstrates, within the French and English settler colonial contexts, exploration and mapmaking were driven by the Discovery Doctrine, which established under European law that explorers "immediately and automatically acquired property rights in native lands," gaining rights over Indigenous inhabitants without the latter's knowledge or consent. Rivers played a major role in this process as the doctrine dictated that the "discovery of the mouth of the river gave the discovering country a claim over all the lands drained by that river." This made inland waterways a primary vehicle of colonization, a fact that sheds new light on Louis Joliet and Jacques Marquette's so-called discovery of the Mississippi in 1673, as well as on Thomas Jefferson's imperial ambitions and his sponsoring of the 1804–1806 Lewis and Clark Expedition into the Louisiana and Pacific Northwest territories via western rivers.[6] In direct opposition to colonial mapping and its logic of conquest, Goeman's concept of Indigenous "(re)mapping" uses narrative and remembering to highlight tribal continuity and connections between stories, peoples, and places, creating a space in which cultural memory and land come together. Her approach describes geography not in terms of ownership but relationships—to the land and to each other, to the past and to the future.[7]

The stories embedded in Harjo's and Erdrich's poetic remembering and remapping enable a continuity that is tied to ancestral homelands along the Mississippi and enacted through the poets' generative act of creation. The page—and in the case of Erdrich's video poem, the frame—invokes further possibilities by building an archive of Indigenous memory and poetic intervention and linking the past, present, and future. The poems highlight the Mississippi to articulate Native presence in the South and in the interior of the continent and retheorize the notion of Indigenous space in a way that defies colonial mapping. Both writers transcend regional and temporal boundaries, following the flow of the river to provide a broader definition of Indigenous homelands.[8] They produce written records for future generations, passing on ancestral cultural memory and stories. In the words of Goeman, Native stories strengthen communities by speaking "to a storied land and storied peoples, connecting generations to particular locales and in a web of relationships."[9]

Harjo and Erdrich both lead the reader away from settler cities and toward other kinds of geographical features, presenting the river as a more complete depository of Indigenous memory. Harjo's poem reroutes its attention from New Orleans as a settler city to the river that made it. Thinking in terms of mud, layers, and blood, Harjo connects the Lower Mississippi to post-Removal Oklahoma via embodied memory. Erdrich moves away from colonial centers of power on the East Coast by turning inland to the Indigenous Mississippi, highlighting the river instead of Minneapolis as a city that paved over its Indigenous homelands. In both poems, the river becomes a "memoryscape," a landscape that acts as a "conduit connecting past, present, and future."[10]

By centering their remappings on rivers, Harjo's and Erdrich's poems reclaim Indigenous waterways as conveyors of Native memory. As transportation routes and connectors, rivers both predate colonization and evade private ownership and state control. Filled with stories and ancestral memories that bridge millennia, they theorize and enact the kind of Native cartography and poetic remappings Goeman writes about. Focusing on the historically important space of the Mississippi River allows Harjo and Erdrich to access Native histories, presents, and futures that are rooted in place but never static. The river serves as a vehicle of Indigenous memory and continuity, connecting two seemingly disparate contemporary and historical Indigenous centers in the Great Lakes Region and the Gulf South.

## The Delta: Bulbancha / New Orleans

Joy Harjo's "New Orleans," published in 1983, centers Native people by focusing on the landscape of the Mississippi, which curves around the old French Quarter before merging with the Gulf of Mexico further south at the river's delta. Searching for Indigenous histories, the poem finds them absent from the settler city and turns instead to the river to draw connections between Native stories, people, and places. Playing with the themes of time and memory, Harjo's poem moves between contemporary New Orleans with its colonial monuments and architecture and the earth towns in which the Creeks lived when they made contact with Hernando de Soto, the sixteenth-century Spanish conquistador credited with discovering the Mississippi. "New Orleans" aims to remap the public memory of southern Louisiana by highlighting Native histories that official narratives erase while casting colonial history in blue stone, to use an image from Harjo's poem.

Starting with the speaker's futile search for "evidence/ of other Creeks" in the center of the settler city, "New Orleans" moves away from enshrined colonial histories toward the Mississippi River.[11] From its opening lines,

"New Orleans" establishes a relationship between Native people and waterways, playing on the aural ambiguity of the Creeks' name to connect them to the geographical feature in which the speaker eventually locates ancestral memories.[12]

With its appearance, origin, and location, the image of the blue horse made of stone that dominates the first stanza of the poem invokes the intersecting strands of European colonization by Spain, France, and later, the emerging United States. Those familiar with New Orleans will immediately recognize the statue as that of Andrew Jackson, whose violent policies removed Native people west of the Mississippi and enabled the spread of plantation slavery. The fact that the city placed the monument depicting the statesman in his military prowess while reviewing the troops in the Battle of New Orleans in 1814 on the east bank of the river positions Jackson both as a conqueror and a protector of the colonial city. Harjo's poem juxtaposes the preservation of Jackson's legacy on full display in colonial New Orleans with the public invisibility of Native people.[13]

Rewriting the story of place, the poem casts the history of the city in terms that center Indigenous People even as it paints an unexpected picture of Andrew Jackson's statue in the square named after him. "New Orleans" never names the man who led the genocidal charge against the Muscogee Nation in the Muscogee War of 1813–1814 and signed the Indian Removal Act of 1830 once he became president.[14] Instead, it focuses on the animal that carries him, the colonial horse that was reintroduced to the New World in the 1500s. The sudden form shift to a significantly shorter stanza with indented lineation signals a reversal; the word choice in the prominent end position of both lines pairs "horse" with "crazy," invoking Crazy Horse in a subtle allusion. Apart from evaluating Jackson's power-hungry state of mind, the move from the unnamed colonial soldier and statesman to the Lakota warrior who fought against the colonial takeover of Native territory in the Great Plains in the northern part of the Mississippi's watershed rhetorically recenters Indigenous People north and south.[15]

Since the publication of the poem in the early 1980s, Native Americans in Louisiana have made significant strides in visibility and self-presentation, but Jackson's monument still occupies the French Quarter in 2022 despite activist efforts to remove it.[16] While the city has begun reckoning with its Confederate history, it continues to monumentalize Jackson and celebrate Thomas Jefferson's 1803 Louisiana Purchase, an acquisition that prompted the U.S. settler expansion west of the Mississippi, the ethnic cleansing of the Native peoples of the Southeast, and the importation of plantation slavery into the Mississippi River Valley.[17] Even as mounting political pressure is forcing New Orleans to rethink some of its most prominent symbols of white supremacy, its thriving tourism industry continues to capitalize on antebellum nostalgia and the city's colonial culture, thus burying its Native past in the process.

Writing in the Reagan era before such debates ever entered public consciousness, Harjo accesses Indigenous history by turning away from official monuments that only tell the colonial version of history. In her representation, the river is filled with spirits of ancestors as well as of children that are yet to be born (their voices "buried in the Mississippi mud") and allows her to access a history that the very name of the city obfuscates.[18]

Before it was called New Orleans, this space was known as Bulbancha, a meeting place for different Native tribes including the Chitimacha, Houma, Chawasha, Washa, Acolapissa, Tunica-Biloxi, Bayogoula, Natchez, Taensa, and Atakapa-Ishak. A Choctaw name that translates as "a place of many tongues," Bulbancha is an apt name for neutral territory where different bodies of water and over forty distinct tribes came together.[19] According to some sources, "Bulbancha" and its variants were also the names used by the Choctaws and the Chickasaws for the Lower Mississippi, which confirms the historic centrality of the river to this place.[20] Before the various waves of displacement, some West, some South, Bulbancha and the space of the Lower Mississippi served as an Indigenous network space where Native tribes lived and traded. After the colonial invasion, historian Daniel Usner demonstrates, Native Americans maintained ceremonial and trade grounds within settler New Orleans in the seventeenth and eighteenth centuries and continued to populate the city after Jackson's removal policies of the 1830s significantly reduced their numbers. Even as Choctaw women appeared regularly in images of New Orleans market scenes from the last decades of the nineteenth century, the "tragic theme of vanishing Indians almost always framed words and pictures that described—albeit in a limited fashion—actual evidence of Indian resilience and resourcefulness."[21]

To center Native people and counter popular settler extinction tropes, Harjo's poem moves from the city toward the immortal Mississippi, a river that continues to flood and persist in its efforts to change its course and eventually circumvent New Orleans, defying settler logic and the many engineering efforts to control it.[22] Juxtaposing different water images, the poem describes an "endless ocean voyage" to measure the vast distance conquistadors and settlers had to travel by water, marking their remove from the space they have come to occupy. At the same time, the poem plays on the homonymous properties of the Creeks' name to tie them to the river in the heart of New Orleans. Unlike monuments erected by cities and state governments, the river preserves stories, histories, and traces in its sediment, serving as a living, ever-evolving monument. If the statue caught in blue stone is static, in other words, the river is both malleable and adaptable, which signals the discrepancy between official state histories and the ones engraved into the landscape.

With its varying line length and occasional indentation in short stanzas, the free verse "New Orleans" produces riverlike swerves that visually mimic the curves of the river, mapping it onto the page. Signaling logical reversals, these swerves stage an argument between the speaker's remembering and the rest of the city, which seems intent on forgetting Native history while monumentalizing the city's colonial past.

Although the first stanza suggests that Jackson's horse was silenced by being cast into stone, the lines that follow posit that the rocks themselves possess a different memory, linking them to the river as well as to the speaker via her own memory, which "swims deep in blood,/ a delta in the skin. It swims out of Oklahoma,/ deep the Mississippi River."[23] By switching from the memory held by rocks to that embodied in herself, the speaker connects memory with the body, geography, and poetry, blurring the boundaries between them. The river moves the speaker physically, but it also acts as her bloodline, propelling her metrical feet and shaping the poem whose form reflects the meandering Mississippi. Tying poetry to place, the line that describes the river carrying her "feet to these places" positions the poem as a major vehicle of the speaker's reclaiming of the space of New Orleans and of Indigenous history that has been erased from public memory. The stanza analogizes the movement of people and memory, both of which are nonlinear, to the river known for changing its course and shifting its riverbed.[24]

Harjo's visualization of the river insists that readers turn away from the settler city and its public monuments to the Mississippi itself. Since the river predates the colonial architecture of New Orleans, it acts as a more accurate depository for the memory of Creek presence. At the same time, the image of a "delta in the skin" maps geography onto the body, highlighting Indigenous People's links to the land by drawing connections between rivers and blood as two essential life forces. The speaker compares ancestral memories encoded in the body to the Mississippi River delta south of New Orleans, a striking landform created by sediment deposition. The poem's image of the body as land shows the two as inextricably linked, but it also connects Creeks' ancestral lands along the Lower Mississippi with their postrelocation territory in Oklahoma, articulating a more fluid and relational cartography. Rerouting the reader's focus from a city filled with colonial monuments to the river that made it, the poet uses images of mud, layers, and blood to connect ancestral Creek lands along the Lower River to postremoval Creek territory in Oklahoma via embodied memory, expanding the notion of Indigenous homelands.

These images connect the three elements of literary scholar Chadwick Allen's "blood/land/memory complex," which highlights the centrality of land to Indigenous identities (i.e., blood) and the process of reimagining erased Indigenous histories (i.e., memory). Harjo's lines name blood as the biological link that transmits Indigenous memory on the one hand and as an indicator of the violence that propelled the movement of people from lands along the Lower Mississippi to Oklahoma on the other.[25] The river as a conveyor of Native memory is central to the poem's remapping, a notion the speaker cements with the only line repetition in the poem, noting twice that her spirit drinks from the river.

"New Orleans" formally enacts a layered structure that mirrors the depth of Indigenous presence and ultimately restores Native people to their central status at the surface and not just at the bottom layers of time, the river, and the poem itself. In this way, it emphasizes the relations between different periods and geographical locales, as well as between ancestors and posterity. The poem creates a formal visualization of the sedimented histories along the Mississippi, first presenting the river as a grave for hundreds of Creeks and, later, for Hernando de Soto.

The speaker's memory and the poem itself carry forward the voices that the lines describe as buried in the Mississippi mud, contributing to an Indigenous future. By giving visibility to Native presence in New Orleans and claiming lost territory through the act of writing, the speaker resists the erasure and dispossession attempted by relocation and asserts the Creeks' claim to the Southeast. Through the metaphor of the river as blood and vice versa, the poem describes homelands as carried in the body on the one hand, and the landscape as always carrying the memory of former inhabitants on the other. Placing the Lower Mississippi in relation to the temporally and geographically removed Creeks in Oklahoma, the poem remaps the river as Indigenous space, emphasizing the continuity between different locations as well as between the past, present, and future. The remapping of the river as filled with Indigenous voices and embodied memories brings such histories to the surface and offsets the erasures of the urban landscape of downtown New Orleans. In the words of literary scholar Tracey Watts, the New Orleans of the poem is both "sensuous and animate," harboring "memories of a precolonial past that persists into contemporary daily life," although it might be more accurate to attribute these qualities to the river rather than the city proper.[26]

The line breaks in this section of the poem reinforce the idea of layering, formally enacting a sedimentary structure that mimics the muddy deposits on the river's banks yet blurs any real separation between the layers. The enjambments mimic the burial in terms of river depth and the passing of time: buried at the bottom are the voices, indicating another type of silencing that the poem counteracts with its own lines and feet. In the order of reading, the voices of the past are at the very bottom of the river bed and most deeply buried in the past, persisting despite the many efforts to erase them; the real and metaphorical remains of ancestors and lost future generations are in the prominent middle; the river current and cruise ships are on the surface, ignoring what lies beneath and creating their own narrative; and most crucially, stories made of memory are at the very top, occupying the realm of the present. All these temporal layers are present at any given moment; since orality is at the center of the first and the last layers, the poem suggests that stories and poetry are what keeps this memory and generational persistence alive. What literary scholar Nancy Lang has called the "ongoing, multilayered and multivocal memories" of Harjo's poems blurs the gap between different temporal levels and the Indigenous People of the past, present, and future, while the blurring of layers signals the fact that the consequences of removal and erasure persist to this day.[27] The final striking image of "pleasure boats" on the surface of the river contrasts the violent history of Native displacement with the ongoing popularity of luxury steamboats like the *Delta Queen* and the *American Queen*, pointing to the ways in which different forms of nostalgia tourism and official state commemorations build on a distorted partial history rooted in the erasure of Native people.

The memory that has long lingered in the landscape now exists on the page in a written record as well: "here" on the page and beyond the text in the Mississippi mud; along the banks mirrored by the shape of the poem and along the Lower Mississippi. With the "here" of the final line of the layered stanza discussed above, Harjo refers both to the context of the poem and outside it to historical events that shaped the lives of her ancestors along the Lower River. In 1837, a steamboat explosion known as the Monmouth Disaster killed hundreds of Creeks in a Mississippi River accident just north of Baton Rouge during one of the forced removals to the western territories now known as the Trail of Tears. For Harjo, "here" marks historically significant time and space and points to the generative potential of poetry. The opening image of Mississippi mud endows the "here" with a different history than the frequent colonial accounts of the river that privilege European conquest; according to Creek creation myths, the first human beings emerged from the underground, possibly from clay.[28] In tying Creek voices to Mississippi mud, the poem claims these origins as well as the physical landscape of the Lower River.

By turning toward the river and away from monuments honoring architects of dispossession like Jackson, Harjo's poem remembers the Creek casualties of American territorial expansionism, locating their bodies and telling their story through the speaker. The foregrounding of the Mississippi exposes the historical omissions over which cruise tourism that capitalizes on antebellum nostalgia tends to glide, highlighting the profound irony of blood being the driving force behind pleasure. Despite this image of death, the poem's focus on stories made of memory privileges survivance, to borrow the concept of writer and scholar Gerald Vizenor (Minnesota Chippewa Tribe, White Earth Reservation), countering colonial narratives of erasure and acting as a practice of resistance.[29] By reestablishing the Native Mississippi on the page and mapping it onto the speaker as a linked conveyor of Indigenous memory, the poem also acts restoratively. The speaker's embodiment of generational memory and ancestral geography and the act of the poem's creation point to survival and continuity on the one hand and contribute to an Indigenous future on the other.

Looking for material evidence that would validate her memory, the speaker turns to de Soto, whom she claims to remember, the verb choice indicating that she carries embodied ancestral memories within herself. Positing that de Soto was drowned by the Creeks, the speaker searches for his body to validate her remembering and, paradoxically, speak to Creek history along the Lower River.[30] While colonial sources agree that de Soto died on the banks of the river, some disagreement exists about how the death occurred, with mainstream historical accounts usually having him succumb to a fever, secretly dropped in the river by his own men.[31] Instead, Harjo's poem presents the gold-thirsty de Soto as drowned by the Creeks. Still, de Soto's fantasy of streets made of precious metals where he could dance with ladies in silk comes to life in contemporary New Orleans with its lace, silk, and silver.

While the bones of de Soto buried in the river's bottom would validate Creek accounts of history, the settler city with its system of monuments and colonial architecture speaks to the Spaniard's survival. The images conjured up by Harjo's adjectives create parallels between the two worlds, drawing attention to the fact that de Soto's vision outlived the conquistador himself. On the one hand, these lines invoke the lopsidedness of historical preservation and the irony of having to look for the colonizer's body to give validity to the memory of one's ancestors. On the other, they highlight the fact that although de Soto might be dead, the legacies set in motion by his conquest persist, and present-day New Orleans bears many markers of colonialism in its architecture and urban layout. The poem's description of above-ground stone crypts and mausoleums built on swampy ground come to literalize the persistence of the past into the present.

The racialized imagery of Black mammy dolls in the last lines of the stanza discussed above widens the poem's perspective on the city's history, nodding to the intertwined histories of dispossession for African American and Indigenous Peoples, which Harjo explores in more detail in the opening pages of her memoir *Crazy Brave*. The fact that in the early eighteenth century, Native Americans who labored alongside enslaved African Americans accounted for almost a quarter of the city's enslaved population speaks to the overlapping histories of the two groups in New Orleans.[32] Responding to the city's whitewashed façade, "New Orleans" with its layered imagery draws on the tradition of Southern Gothic literature to expose the ways in which the Crescent City paved over much of its history, performing a live burial of sorts. With its French architecture and antebellum statues, the old center at the time of Harjo's writing was a monument to the colonizer's civilization, one that preserved the past only in the revisionist act of "careful remembering and necessary forgetting," to quote Civil War historian David Blight.[33]

"New Orleans" connects the absence of de Soto's body to the existence of the settler city, indicating that he might have survived. The poem ends with a sighting of the sixteenth-century conquistador in the guise of a tourist drinking on Bourbon Street while dancing with a woman, described with the same adjectives as the "mad and crazy" statue of Jackson's horse with which the poem opens, which connects de Soto to Jackson as well as to the common American. In the poem's interpretation of history, colonialism is embodied both in de Soto and in the image of a tourist, suggesting that the settler system of monuments, antebellum tourist mementos, and visitors who are intent on extracting pleasure from the city are all implicated in the colonial project.[34]

Like the dramatic indentation of everything but the first line in the poem's final stanza, the woman's skin color, associated with both the gold for which de Soto was searching and the river bottom where he was rumored to meet his demise, suggests a final reversal and a delayed realization of the colonist's burial. The poem's open ending suggests a continuity that goes beyond the earlier wish for Indigenous voices and "tobacco brown bones" walking around the old center of New Orleans.[35] Through the image of the gold-colored dancing woman and her own witnessing of de Soto, the speaker demonstrates proof of the "evidence of other Creeks" she sought out in the poem's first stanza. The poem, in other words, gives a voice to Indigenous memory and creates the record for which the speaker longed, as well as getting the last word on de Soto's fate.

Even as the speaker returns to the city, the final image the poem offers is of the river, which contains the memories and histories that she was unable to find in settler New Orleans. Unlike the lace, silk, and gold that characterize the colonial architecture of the city, the mud of the river's bottom invokes both Creek creation myths and their dwellings—the visual pause before the poem's denunciation of the Spaniards' favorite metal earlier in the poem emphasizes the contrast between the two: "The Creeks lived in earth towns, / not gold."[36] At the same time, the river harbors ancestral spirits and fuels the speaker's poetry by carrying her feet to ancestral homelands along the Lower River, providing a window into Indigenous histories along its banks.

## The Source: Minneapolis–St. Paul

While Harjo's poem centers Indigenous lands along the Lower Mississippi close to the river's delta, Heid E. Erdrich's "Pre-Occupied" (2013) focuses on the northern part of the Mississippi watershed near its headwaters. The poem addresses extraction from Indigenous lands along the Upper River and its tributaries and links environmental issues to a critique of the Occupy Wall Street Movement and its ignorance of Indigenous forms of dispossession.[37] If Harjo's 1983 poem turns to the river to find evidence of Indigenous histories that colonial New Orleans erased, Erdrich's centers the Mississippi to draw links between the health of the watershed and the longevity and perseverance of Indigenous tribes along its banks, arguing for a future based on reciprocity and sustainability rather than extraction. Erdrich insists on the interconnectedness of colonialism and modern capitalism, both of which are based on extraction, whether of land, labor, or natural resources. Her poem exists in textual as well as video versions; the latter was produced by Erdrich, codirected by her and Vincent Moniz Jr. (NuuÉtaare tribal member and enrolled citizen of the Three Affiliated Tribes on the Ft. Berthold Indian Reservation), and art directed and animated by Jonathan Thunder (Red Lake Ojibwe).[38] "Pre-Occupied" remaps and reclaims the Mississippi as Indigenous space, outlining the river in its relation to Native people, their history, and their present. The video poem in particular, which establishes the Mississippi as a site of artistic collaboration, revives the historically significant role of the river to Native life and culture in its watershed by representing it in relation to historical and contemporary Indigenous experiences along its banks.

Erdrich and the team of artists who created the video poem populate its space with a postmodern collage of voices, images, historical events, and popular culture references. The video poem opens with footage of St. Anthony Falls on the Mississippi River in downtown Minneapolis and the voice of African American poet Langston Hughes reading "The Negro Speaks of Rivers." As Erdrich starts reciting the poem, Hughes's voice continues to loop in the background. This layering is reinforced in the language and the visual components of the video poem, which invoke the Occupy Movement, the oil industry's environmental extraction on Indigenous lands, and Superman, the all-American hero as he appears in the 1942 cartoon *Electric Earthquake* and the 1991 rock hit "Superman's Song" by the Crash Test Dummies. The animation also features art by Carolyn Lee Anderson (Navajo), Angela Erdrich (Turtle Mountain Ojibwe), and Andrea Carlson—the artist whose work I describe in the beginning of this essay—providing a platform for the showcasing of multimedia contemporary Indigenous art. "Pre-Occupied" remaps the space of the river by foregrounding Indigenous stories and characterizing the waterway in terms of relationships and reciprocity instead of ownership, discursively reclaiming the territory from the settler occupation that started with colonial mapmaking. The many narrative associations that structure Erdrich's poem mimic the flow of the river with its many tributaries, presenting it as intertwined with Indigenous memory and suggesting that the health and future of both are inextricably linked.

Erdrich's poem is invested in a recuperation of Indigenous memory; its title already questions dominant historical narratives by pointing to the fact that the North American continent was populated long before settler occupation. Drawing on the irony of the catchy percentages used by Occupy Wall Street activists—the fact that, as Erdrich's endnote to the poem tells us, Indigenous People today comprise about 1 percent of the U.S. population, making them "more or less, the original 1% as well as the original 100%"—"Pre-Occupied" critiques the omission of Native Americans from the agenda of those the Occupy movement represents as the 99 percent.[39] Replacing images of Ojibwe wigwams with modern tents used in the Occupy Movement, the poem plays on the ambiguity of the word "bank," which denotes the institution at the heart of Occupy's critique as well as the physical landscape of the waterway.

"Pre-Occupied" draws connections between colonial land theft and the financial crisis of 2008, using the metaphor of the river to connect seemingly disparate places and periods. It moves from contemporary images of downtown Minneapolis to a depiction of the prehistoric river as a place of genesis; from pipelines leading to tar sands in Canada to the East Coast Hudson River as presented in 1940s pop culture; from the settler Occupy Movement in 2011 to the Indigenous occupation of Alcatraz in 1969 and Wounded Knee in 1973. The speaker's digressions force the audience to follow her associative jumps and forge their own connections between them. As literary critic Stephanie LeMenager puts it, rivers generally serve as both symbolic and material links in that they "connect us and carry our refuse through space and time," providing a narrative through line.[40]

In "Pre-Occupied," the river, like the poem, is characterized by a multi-directional flow: "Flow flow flow both ways in time/ There's a river to consider after all."[41] Bracketed by a triple repetition of the word "river" in its first and penultimate lines, the poem relies on rivers to connect the majority of the speaker's associations. The dual meaning of the word "bank" first links the river to Occupy Wall Street; the jump east is made by juxtaposing the Mississippi with the Hudson River; and tributaries to the Missouri, which itself empties into the Mississippi, connect locations along the northern half of the Keystone pipeline as well as the site of Wounded Knee. In text and on film, Erdrich's river brings together Indigenous histories and contemporary Native art to unsettle settler activism, claiming the space from which the Occupy movement excludes Native people.

The Mississippi River and the space around Minneapolis are central to the remappings of the textual and the video poems. Located on the banks of the Mississippi, Minneapolis has the importance of the river encoded in its name, which derives from a Dakota word for water (mni) and the Greek word for city (polis).[42] As literary scholar Laura Furlan points out: "Located within a deeper sense of time, to riff on Wai Chee Dimock's term, Minneapolis is Indian Territory."[43] Minnesota has been inhabited by the Dakota, Cheyenne, Ho Chunk, and beginning approximately A.D. 900, the Anishinaabe or Ojibwe. National Native organizations in Minneapolis date back to the 1920s, and the city is also the birthplace of the American Indian Movement (AIM), the grassroots movement for Indigenous rights founded in 1968, which gained national recognition with the occupation of Alcatraz between 1969 and 1971.[44]

If the Minneapolis of the late twentieth century might have been more visible as a modern Indigenous center than New Orleans thanks to activist efforts, legacies of the late nineteenth and the early twentieth centuries persist. During that time, the settler city paved over, dynamited, and erased from memory much of the deep history Furlan writes about. Instances include the destruction of two sacred Dakota sites intimately tied to the Mississippi: Spirit Island, which I discuss in the introduction, and Wakáŋ Tipi. In the 1880s, a railroad company dynamited the entrance to the sacred Wakáŋ Tipi cave and its petroglyphs, which stood by what later became known as the Indian Mounds Park by the banks of the Mississippi in St. Paul, to make way for train tracks after the Treaty of 1837 took the cave from the Dakota. Shortly after, a brewery started using the water for beer production and used the site for storage, gradually transforming it into "a desecrated dumping ground for railroad rubbish, toxic waste and used household goods."[45] Of the six caves that existed at Wakáŋ Tipi, four were dynamited, and the larger remaining one was renamed after the first European who encountered it, becoming known as Carver's Cave.[46] Additionally, thirty-one out of the thirty-seven surrounding mounds were bulldozed "in the name of development for a better view; the oak savannah was destroyed and the wetlands were drained and poisoned."[47]

Such actions are far from isolated anomalies; they reflect processes of settler extraction and destruction of Indigenous lands that unfold all over the continent. As environmental historian Traci Voyles points out in her analysis of "wastelanding" in the context of uranium mining in Navajo country, "the logic of settler colonialism denies that its 'wastelands' could be sacred, could be claimed, could have a history, or could be thought of as home." Instead, those places are marked as "empty except for Indians" and made into "sacrificial land."[48] In their published work on Wakáŋ Tipi, Odawa/Ojibwe and Dakota activists/scholars Roxanne Gould and Jim Rock describe the process of reclaiming the land at Wakáŋ Tipi by "reengaging the memory of the Dakota relationship to the place" and reintroducing its Indigenous name. Since 2018, the Lower Phalen Creek Project, an organization working on restoring the site, has been developing the Wakáŋ Tipi cultural and environmental interpretive center, which will tell the story of this place from the perspective of Dakota voices.[49]

Like in Bulbancha/New Orleans, extraction and erasure in the Twin Cities work on material and rhetorical levels, expunging Native histories from public memory and official state narratives, so art becomes an important way of subverting such rhetoric. A particularly striking instance of the violence reproduced by place names can be found at Bdote, a Dakota sacred place where the Haha Wakpa and Mni Sota Wakpa—the Mississippi and Minnesota rivers—meet. Bdote is not just a sacred site but a place of genesis: "We are told that we were brought here to this land from the stars to the place where the Minnesota and Mississippi rivers meet."[50] Bdote is now officially a part of the Fort Snelling State Park, named after the 1819 U.S. military structure that held the displaced and imprisoned Dakota survivors of the Dakota War of 1862.[51] The surviving Dakota prisoners, as historian William Millikan shows, financed much of the growth of Minnesota by being forced or tricked into giving away their scrip, the certificate entitling them to the possession of their lands, which ensured the white takeover of land in the Dakota Territory.[52]

The history of colonial violence and erasure of sacred Indigenous spaces along the Mississippi contextualizes Erdrich's centering of the river and her remapping of the space as a site of contemporary Native art and activism. The written poem begins with a triple repetition of the word "river," which is identified halfway through as the Mississippi, mirroring its position in the symbolic if not the geographical middle of the continent. In the video version, the poem opens with a Langston Hughes poem, which I discuss later, and footage of the regulated St. Anthony Falls on the Upper River in downtown Minneapolis. The sound and imagery ground the video poem in Indigenous deep time and in settler modifications to the landscape from the outset. As Erdrich starts reciting the poem, the animation positions the repetitive "river" into a spiral while Hughes's voice continues to loop in the background.

Erdrich's poem starts as a direct address to the river, formally mimicking a flowing waterway as well as the speaker's many digressions, visually connecting the text to the land:

> River      river      river
> I never      never      never
> etched your spiral icon in limestone
> or          for that matter          pitched a tent on cement
> near your banks
>
> Banks of marble          stock still          all movement in the plaza
> river walking its message on the avenue
> rallied in bitter wind
>
> Excuse my digression      my mind tends . . .[53]

With the repetition of "never" the speaker distances herself from various acts of colonial occupation, giving the poem the shape of the river to signal her ancestors' embeddedness in its geography. The triple structure built on repetition, slant rhymes, and wide spacing reproduces on the page the shape of the river flowing between its banks, etching its way into the landscape as it has for millennia. The varying line length that produces the undulating right-hand border is drawn out because of the spacing. This approximates the ebbs and flows of a river, as well as the digressive meanders of the speaker's own thoughts, which constantly traverse time periods and geographies. The poet's musings move from the interior of the continent to both coasts via Manhattan and Alcatraz and blend the contemporary moment with Indigenous activism from the middle of the twentieth century as well as with the prehistoric river as an origin point for Indigenous People.

In its remapping, "Pre-Occupied" tells the story of the interior and of Native American history in the heart of the continent:

> River      river      river          Our river
> Map of the Milky Way
> reflection of stars
> whence all life commenced

100% of all life on our planet

River in the middle        Mississippi
not the East Coast Hudson where this all started[54]

Although the poem invokes the story of East Coast colonization via its critique of Occupy, its imagery shifts inward toward the Mississippi, reclaiming the space that served as a marker of Indigenous removal. Instead of
dwelling on Dutch colonization via the Hudson in the early 1600s "where all
this started," Erdrich focuses on a Mississippi River situated in Indigenous
time and space. While the video poem visually identifies the unnamed river
of the poem's opening lines as the Mississippi from the outset, the textual
version does not do so until the middle of the poem. The opening footage
foregrounds settler modifications to the river by focusing on the engineered
spillway that replaced the natural St. Anthony Falls in the nineteenth century, but the lines above modify the river with a first-person plural pronoun
("Our river"), shifting from an individual to a collective account of the Mississippi's role in Indigenous culture. Giving life to "100% of all life on our
planet," the river is directly linked to the people defined in an earlier line
as "we original 100%," the repetition of the percentage establishing a clear
correlation. The invocation of the Milky Way links the Mississippi and Indigenous Peoples to the stars, painting them all as original. As a primordial
element, stars figure prominently in Native creation stories. The poem's frequent repetition of the word "consider"—"There is a river to consider" acts
as a refrain in the poem—plays on its derivation from the Latin *sidus* for star
or constellation.

This longue-durée perspective of Native life along the Mississippi is crucial to the reclaiming and remapping that take place in the poem. Like the
river, the spiral, a recurring motif in the video poem and one of the first
images invoked in the textual version, serves as a helpful visualization of
the poem's historicized view that is nevertheless focused on the present
and continues into the future. In literary scholar Lisa Brooks's theorization,
the origins of the spiral embedded in place "lie in the ancient worlds, but
it moves through our own bodies in the present, perhaps with a sense of
irony."[55] The video poem uses both the spiral and the river to connect historical Indigenous presence to contemporary Native art and activism, highlighting the continuity between them. In the words of literary scholar Susan
Bernardin, this "riverine mixed-media form," marked by "collaborative aesthetics," is yet another aspect of "the work's riverine metaphor of Indigenous interconnectivity across time and space."[56]

The primacy of the river and forms of collaboration it engenders are reinforced in the video poem, in which the footage of the technologically altered

landscape of St. Anthony Falls transitions to a hand-drawn map of star-reflecting water in the same portion of the Upper Mississippi. The image, taken from *Stories from St. Anthony #3*, a 2010 mixed-media piece by Carolyn Lee Anderson (Navajo), appears in tandem with Erdrich's repetition of the word "river" and the phrase "Map of the Milky Way." Like the textual and video poem versions of "Pre-Occupied," Anderson's image, combined with short text conveying a highly personalized contemporary story, asserts the importance of the present and puts the Mississippi and the natural world surrounding it at the center of its micro-universe.[57]

The visual, sonic, and textual focus on the river and the video poem's collaborative aesthetics expand the poem's reach geographically as well as temporally. The poem claims the space of the river by characterizing it not in terms of ownership and the settler logic of maps but in terms of relationships and reciprocity, as is made clear by the variation of the same line in the first and the second half of the poem: "There's a river to consider after all" and later, "There's a river that considers us after all." The small shift speaks to the ethics of accountability and sustainability absent from the logic of profit-driven imperial expansion.

"Pre-Occupied" remaps the Mississippi as Indigenous space, but not in a proprietary way that would deny other groups' experiences with the river as it moves through space and time. Perhaps the most significant difference between the textual and the video poems is the addition of Langston Hughes in the latter. The animation opens with a recording of the Harlem Renaissance poet's famous refrain from "The Negro Speaks of Rivers;" Hughes's voice remains in the background even as Erdrich starts her own recital, deepening her timbre as well as the history of the Mississippi she conjures up: "I've known rivers:/ Ancient, dusky rivers.// My soul has grown deep like the rivers."[58] According to Hughes's autobiography, he wrote the poem in 1920 at the age of seventeen after crossing the Mississippi at St. Louis on a train ride toward Mexico to visit his father.[59] Hughes recalls the Mississippi's role in the slave trade as well as in freedom and emancipation; he explains in his autobiography that the poem was inspired by an article he read about a young Abraham Lincoln's two flatboat trips down the Mississippi to New Orleans in 1828 and 1831, which allegedly made him vow to end slavery.[60] As Bernardin points out, the sonic layering of Erdrich's and Hughes's voices and the frequent repetition of the word "river" in the poem convey "the river's role as structuring metaphor and mnemonic device" and signal toward "the deep racial and national histories" invoked by the Mississippi.[61] The river, in other words, both possesses a memory of its own and makes others remember, performing the same kind of work as it does in Harjo's "New Orleans."

Hughes's voice adds to the sprawling temporal dimensions of "Pre-Occupied" by zooming out and providing a global perspective on the localized issues of dispossession the video poem addresses. "The Negro Speaks of Rivers" connects the Euphrates, the Congo, the Nile, and the Mississippi—Middle Eastern, African, and American rivers and consequently the people of the African diaspora—through time and space in an affirmative ode to Blackness. Invoking Hughes's pattern by repeating the generic "river" before focusing on the Indigenous waterway at the heart of the poem—"River    river    river        Our    river"—"Pre-Occupied" relies on Hughes's words to provide an African American perspective on the history of the Mississippi, pointing to the intertwining of different forms of colonial violence and exploitation along the same river.[62]

The video poem's positioning of the voices of Erdrich and Hughes to speak together creates bridges between Native American and African American experiences of imperial violence along the Mississippi and traditions of poetic resistance. The lag in their synchronization also points to crucial differences, weaving a complex narrative of dispossession that goes beyond Harjo's image of New Orleans as a city marketing its colonial architecture and nostalgic white fantasy by selling "black mammy dolls/ holding white babies."[63] While Lincoln was instrumental in abolishing slavery with his Emancipation Proclamation on January 1, 1863, his government committed many atrocities against Native Americans, most notably the Dakota after the war of 1862. On December 26, 1862, just days before he issued his most famous presidential proclamation, Lincoln signed another executive order to hang thirty-eight Dakota men at Mankato, Minnesota, which remains "the largest, simultaneous mass hanging from one gallows in world history."[64]

Following the narrative arc provided by the flow of the river, the video poem moves between historical land dispossession and contemporary environmental extractivism, presenting them as interrelated. The speaker elaborates on her refusal to provide sustenance for mainstream white society—characterized as the 99 percent—the way Native Americans did for the first settler colonists, stating that she is "a bit pre-occupied" and turning to contemporary environmental extraction from Native lands instead:

> Simply distracted by sulfide emissions    tar sands        pipelines.        Foster care        polar bears.        Hydro-fracking.    And the playlist deeply intoning *Superman never made any money*[65]

Quoting the Crash Test Dummies' 1991 hit "Superman's Song," Erdrich contrasts the bleak environmental exploitation of the capitalist state with the performatively altruistic, quintessentially American superhero, who comes to stand in for the state. The poem exposes the clash between America's self-presentation and its long history of removing, displacing, erasing, and suppressing Indigenous Peoples and making profits off Native land. On one level, the line break between "foster" and "care" instructs us to pay attention to environmental issues and see them in relation to capitalism. On another, the phrase reminds us that throughout the nineteenth and the early twentieth centuries, the state tried to culturally eliminate Indigeneity by placing Native children in boarding schools and foster care in the name of assimilation. Like the state itself, the Occupy movement's critique of capitalism did little to consider Native Americans, upon whose displacement the American empire is predicated.[66]

The spacing reinforces such associative digressions, inviting readers to construct their own meaning and make connections between different issues of cultural (mis)representation, land occupation, and environmental atrocities that the poem—like the river—brings together. The environmental atrocities listed in Erdrich's poem are a contemporary manifestation of long-standing patterns of dispossession and extraction: sulfide emissions coming from oil and natural gas extraction and processing; the high-risk practice of hydro-fracking; tar sands and the pipelines that lace the continent to connect the production, processing, and consumption of oil and natural gas, often on Indigenous lands and waterways. As Erdrich puts it in one of the poem's concluding endnotes, creating a formal link between poetry and research and dissolving the idea of art being separate from politics: "This era of alternative energy has become the new land grab, the new water grab. Indigenous activists are thoroughly preoccupied with the social and environmental issues I mention and more." The way the U.S. government treats the river, in other words, is rooted in the way it has historically extracted from Native people. Private companies and the settler state keep appropriating Indigenous lands and resources for environmentally hazardous projects like the Keystone and the Dakota Access Pipelines along the tributaries of the Upper Mississippi, and for copper mining and hydro fracking elsewhere.[67]

Intertwining typical environmental injustice concerns with a discussion of the settler colonial land grab—"Pre-Occupied" cites the 1942 cartoon *Electric Earthquake*, in which an Indigenous scientist proclaims that Manhattan rightfully belongs to his people, only to be thwarted by Superman: "Possibly, but just what/ do you expect us to do about it?"—the poem shows the continuity between different forms of extraction and dispossession.[68] The extractive practices to which Erdrich alludes take place in the interior of the continent far from centers of power, on the lands of politically and economically disempowered people. Their peripheral position propels their invisibility, but "Pre-Occupied" resists this erasure by centering Indigenous lands, peoples, art, and activism via its representation of the Mississippi. The poem's listing of environmental atrocities leads to an explicit remapping of the Mississippi as Indigenous space in the very next line: "River     river     river        Our river/ Map of the Milky Way."[69] The sequencing and the emphatic long pause before the possessive pronoun express a tension between the environmental side effects of settler capitalism and the Indigenous river that is considered sacred, suggesting that the health of the watershed is directly tied to Native reclamation of these lands.

Reversing the narrative of colonial occupation through its representation of the river and the forms of Indigenous perseverance and collaboration it engenders, the poem encourages continued Native American resistance, highlighting two of the most well-known examples of Indigenous activists' reclaiming of land from the twentieth century. "Pre-Occupied" ends in an activist call to organize and (re)occupy as images of wigwams return to replace modern tents, and newsclips and photographs of the Native American occupation of Alcatraz and Wounded Knee fill the screen: "Occupy Re-occupy Alcatraz and Wounded Knee."[70]

## Conclusion

Each of the two poems draws connections between histories, people, and places, using narrative and remembering to foreground Indigenous stories and counter colonial erasure. Read together, "New Orleans" and "Pre-Occupied" traverse the three decades and the many miles that separate the Lower and the Upper Mississippi, demonstrating a riverine poetics that mimics the river's flow to enact a relational cartography that defies colonial mapmaking. The poems rhetorically reclaim the historically significant Indigenous space of the Mississippi River Valley and embody on the page a space in which land and cultural memory can come together.

Harjo's and Erdrich's poems create an Indigenous Mississippi, presenting the waterway as a vehicle of Indigenous memory and replacing representations of the river as an icon of the U.S. empire and Westward expansion. Echoing Hughes's line about knowing "rivers ancient as the world and older than the flow of blood in human veins," they invoke the origins of human history to reassert the river as Indigenous space in the present day.[71] Like Andrea Carlson's installation *Uncompromising Hand*, the poems imagine Native futures by activating long-held connections to this space, asserting a contemporary presence, and reinforcing the notion of homelands through their centering of the ancient, continuously regenerating river. In their remappings, both poets turn away from settler cities and their monuments toward rivers, presenting them as depositories of Native stories and memories and suggesting that the health and future of both are closely linked.

SARA ČERNE (Ph.D., English, Northwestern University) is a research grants manager at the University of California Humanities Research Institute. Her work has contributed to a multiyear Humanities Without Walls grant titled "Indigenous Art and Activism in Changing Climates: The Mississippi River Valley, Colonialism, and Environmental Change."

## References

Allen, Chadwick. *Blood Narrative: Indigenous Identity in American Indian and Maori Literary and Activist Texts*. Durham, NC: Duke University Press, 2002.

Anderson, Carolyn Lee, *Stories from St. Anthony #3*, mixed media. Paper card, Minneapolis: Birchbark Books & Native Arts, Minneapolis, 2010

Barker, Joanne. "Territory as Analytic: The Dispossession of Lenapehoking and Subprime Crisis." *Social Text* 36, no. 2 (June 2018): 19–39.

Bernardin, Susan. "'There's a River to Consider': Heid E. Erdrich's 'Pre-Occupied.'" *Studies in American Indian Literatures* 29, no. 1 (Spring 2017): 38–55.

Blee, Lisa, and Jean M. O'Brien. *Monumental Mobility: The Memory Work of Massasoit*. Chapel Hill, NC: University of North Carolina Press, 2019.

Blight, David. *Race and Reunion: The Civil War in American Memory*. Cambridge, MA: Belknap Press, 2001.

Brooks, Lisa. "The Primacy of the Present, the Primacy of Place: Navigating the Spiral of History in the Digital World." *PMLA* 127, no. 2 (March 2012): 308–316.

Byrd, Jodi. *The Transit of Empire: Indigenous Critiques of Colonialism*. Minneapolis: University of Minnesota Press, 2011.

Carlson, Andrea. "On the Uncompromising Hand: Remembering Spirit Island." *Open Rivers: Rethinking Water, Place & Community* 9 (Winter 2018): 63–74. http://editions.lib.umn.edu/openrivers/article/on-the-uncompromising-hand-remembering-spirit-island/.

Darensbourg, Jeffery U., ed. *Bulbancha is Still a Place: Indigenous Culture from New Orleans: The Tricentennial Issue*. Bulbancha: POC Zine Project, 2018.

———. "*Bulbancha is Still a Place: Indigenous Culture from New Orleans: The Language Issue*. Bulbancha: POC Zine Project, 2019.

DeLucia, Christine. "Materialities of Memory: Traces of Trauma and Resilience in Native and Colonial North America." *English Language Notes* 57, no. 2 (2019): 7–21.

Dunbar-Ortiz, Roxanne. *An Indigenous People's History of the United States*. Boston: Beacon, 2014.

Erdrich, Heid E., prod. and codirector. "Pre-Occupied." Codirected by Vincent Moniz Jr., art directed and animated by Jonathan Thunder, 2013. http://heiderdrich.com/video/pre-occupied/.

Erdrich, Heid. E.. "Pre-Occupied." In *Curator of Ephemera at the New Museum for Archaic Media*, 22–24. East Lansing: Michigan State University Press, 2017.

Furlan, Laura M. *Indigenous Cities: Urban Indian Fiction and the Histories of Relocation*. Lincoln: University of Nebraska Press, 2017.

Goeman, Mishuana. "(Re)Mapping Indigenous Presence on the Land in Native Women's Literature." *American Quarterly* 60, no. 2 (June 2008): 295–302.

———. "The Tools of a Cartographic Poet: Unmapping Settler Colonialism in Joy Harjo's Poetry." *Settler Colonial Studies* 2, no. 2 (February 2012): 89–112.

———. *Mark My Words: Native Women Mapping Our Nations.* Minneapolis: University of Minnesota Press, 2013.

Gould, Roxanne, and Jim Rock. "Wakan Tipi and Indian Mounds Park: Reclaiming an Indigenous Feminine Sacred Site." *AlterNative: An International Journal of Indigenous Peoples* 12/3 (September 2016): 224–235.

Grantham, Bill. *Creation Myths and Legends of the Creek Indians.* Gainesville: University of Florida Press, 2002.

Harjo, Joy. "New Orleans." In *How We Became Human: New and Selected Poems: 1975–2001,* 43–46. New York: W.W. Norton & Co, 2008.

Hughes, Langston. *The Big Sea: An Autobiography.* New York: Hill and Wang, 1993.

———. *Weary Blues.* 1926. New York: Alfred A. Knopf, 2015.

Lang, Nancy. "'Twin Gods Bending Over:' Joy Harjo and Poetic Memory." *MELUS* 18, no. 3 (September 1993): 41–49.

LeMenager, Stephanie. *Living Oil: Petroleum Culture in the American Century.* New York: Oxford University Press, 2014.

"Lower Phalen Creek Project—What We Do." Lower Phalen Creek Project Organization, accessed July 7, 2020, https://www.lowerphalencreek.org/whatwedo.

Mack, Dustin J. "The Chickasaws' Place-World: The Mississippi River in Chickasaw History and Geography." *New South* 11 (2018): 1–28.

McPhee, John. "Atchafalaya." *The New Yorker* (February 1987), accessed December 20, 2017, https://www.newyorker.com/magazine/1987/02/23/atchafalaya.

Miller, Robert J. *Native America, Discovered and Conquered: Thomas Jefferson, Lewis and Clark, and Manifest Destiny.* Lincoln: University of Nebraska Press, 2008.

Millikan, William. "The Great Treasure of the Fort Snelling Prison Camp." *Minnesota History* 62, no. 1 (Spring 2010): 4–17.

Pauketat, Timothy R. *Ancient Cahokia and the Mississippians.* Cambridge: Cambridge University Press, 2004.

Schneider, Paul. *Old Man River: The Mississippi River in North American History.* New York: Henry Holt and Company, 2013.

Tuck, Eve, and K. Wayne Yang. "Decolonization is not a Metaphor." *Decolonization: Indigeneity, Education & Society* 1, no. 1 (2012): 1–40.

Usner, Daniel H. *American Indians in Early New Orleans: From Calumet to Raquette.* Baton Rouge: Louisiana State University Press, 2018.

Vizenor, Gerald. *Manifest Manners: Narratives on Postindian Survivance.* Lincoln: University of Nebraska Press, 1999.

Voyles, Traci Brynne. *Wastelanding: Legacies of Uranium Mining in Navajo Country.* Minneapolis: University of Minnesota Press, 2015.

Watts, Tracey. "Haunted Memories: Disruptive Ghosts in the Poems of Brenda

Marie Osbey and Joy Harjo." *The Southern Literary Journal* 46, no. 2 (Spring 2014): 108—127.

Waziyatawin. "Colonial Calibrations: The Expendability of Minnesota's Original People." *William Mitchell Law Review* 39, no. 2 (2013): 450—485.

Wendland, Tegan. "With Lee Statue's Removal, Another Battle of New Orleans Comes to a Close." *NPR* (May 2017), accessed July 3, 2020, https://www.npr.org/2017/05/20/529232823/with-lee-statues-removal-another-battle-of-new-orleans-comes-to-a-close.

Westerman, Gwen and Bruce White. *Mni Sota Makoce: The Land of the Dakota.* St. Paul: Minnesota Historical Society Press, 2012.

## Notes

I would like to thank Northwestern's Center for Native American and Indigenous Studies and the Alice Kaplan Institute for the Humanities as well as the Humanities Without Walls consortium for their generous research support. I am also grateful to Kelly Wisecup and Julia Stern for their tireless guidance and mentorship; to fellow members of the HWW grant for their collaborative spirit; to Jeffery Darensbourg for sharing his insights on Indigenous activism in New Orleans; to Heid E. Erdrich for giving me permission to cite her poem; and to the *NAIS* reviewers and editors for their productive suggestions.

1. Carlson, "On the Uncompromising Hand," 64—65.

2. When referring to Harjo's tribal affiliation, I use the term Muscogee, which the poet uses on her official website (interchangeably spelled as Muscogee and Mvskoke). However, since Harjo uses the term "Creek" throughout her 1983 poem "New Orleans," I do the same when analyzing the poem to maintain consistency with the poet's language. The "Pre-Occupied" video poem was created by Erdrich, Vincent Moniz Jr., and Jonathan Thunder.

3. Goeman, "(Re)Mapping Indigenous Presence on the Land in Native Women's Literature."

4. Byrd, *The Transit of Empire*, xx.

5. Pauketat, *Ancient Cahokia and the Mississippians*, 26.

6. Miller, *Native America, Discovered and Conquered*, 1, 4, 99.

7. Goeman, "(Re)Mapping Indigenous Presence on the Land in Native Women's Literature," 297—301; "The Tools of a Cartographic Poet," 89, 104.

8. Eve Tuck and K. Wayne Yang worry that the focus on decolonizing the mind acts as a "settler move to innocence" because it allows "*conscientization* to stand in for the more uncomfortable task of relinquishing stolen land." Tuck and Yang, "Decolonization is not a Metaphor," 19. In so far as poems as an art form are ever capable of going beyond conscientization, Harjo's and Erdrich's poems do so by making land central to their poetic remappings, rendering the Mississippi in Indigenous time and space.

9. Goeman, *Mark My Words*, 37.

10. DeLucia, "Materialities of Memory," 18.

11. Harjo, "New Orleans," 43.

12. Because of permission issues, I was not able to cite the poem at any length. Harjo's poem can be found in print but her reading of the poem is also available on YouTube.

13. As historians Lisa Blee and Jean M. O'Brien demonstrate, monuments to settler colonialism perform harmful memory work whether they overtly revere colonizers, as Jackson's statue does, or offer images of romanticized premodern Native American archetypes "to underscore frontier mythologies and celebrate the dispossession of the nation's Indigenous inhabitants as a measure of progress." Blee and O'Brien, *Monumental Mobility*, 5, 13.

14. Dunbar-Ortiz, *An Indigenous Peoples' History of the United States*, 100.

15. In an act similar to Harjo's, a 2019 issue of the activist zine *Bulbancha Is Still a Place* features a striking archival image from the Louisiana Research Collection at Tulane University of Jackson's decapitated statue from 1938, reframing public memory and its perception of monuments. Lamenting subsequent repairs, editor Jeffery Darensbourg (Atakapa-Ishak) proclaims in his opening remarks that the collective "we" of Indigenous People in Bulbancha claims full responsibility for the act. *Bulbancha Is Still a Place* revives an ancient place name to assert the primacy of Native people in the area as it celebrates contemporary Indigenous culture from Louisiana. Darensbourg, *Bulbancha is Still a Place*. Explore the zine's website here: http://bulbanchaisstillaplace.org/.

16. In the years following the poem's publication, the city made token efforts to acknowledge Indigenous history and culture, usually in ways that celebrate multiculturalism and deflect from the violence of the colonial enterprise. In 1987, for example, members of various tribes sold crafts and traditional foods in the city's celebration of the drafting of the U.S. Constitution. Usner, *American Indians in Early New Orleans*, 133–134.

17. Between 2015 and 2017, several major Confederate monuments were torn down. In 2017, the city took down the statue of Confederate General Robert E. Lee, which joined the list of other recently removed monuments: the statues of Confederate President Jefferson Davis and Confederate General P.G.T. Beauregard, and the Liberty Place monument, which commemorated a Reconstruction-era attack on the city's integrated police force by white supremacists. Wendland, "With Lee Statue's Removal, Another Battle of New Orleans Comes to a Close."

18. Harjo, 44.

19. Darensbourg, *Bulbancha is Still a Place*.

20. Mack, "The Chickasaws' Place-World," 16.

21. The official census, questionable as its methods for recording underrepresented populations may be, only counted two Native Americans as residents of New Orleans in 1900 but by 1930, the number began slowly but steadily rising. By the 2010s, the census counted over a thousand Native Americans in New Orleans and over thirty thousand in the state of Louisiana. Usner, 93, xv, 2, 6, 94, 130.

22. McPhee, "Atchafalaya."

23. Harjo, 43–44.

24. See Harold Fisk's colorful 1944 maps of the meandering Lower Mississippi, which depict the river's movement in geological time.

25. Allen builds on writer N. Scott Momaday (Kiowa) and his work on "*memory in the blood* or *blood memory*," a trope that "blur[s] distinctions between racial identity (blood) and narrative (memory)" and builds continuity across generations through the process of Indigenous literary production. Allen, *Blood Narrative*, 1, 16, 162.

26. Watts, "Haunted Memories," 109.

27. Lang, "'Twin Gods Bending Over,'" 41.

28. Grantham, *Creation Myths and Legends of the Creek Indians*, 16.

29. Vizenor defines survivance as an "active sense of presence" and a renunciation of "victimry." Vizenor, *Manifest Manners*, vii.

30. Harjo, 45.

31. Schneider, *Old Man River*, 71.

32. Usner cites the 1721 census, which recorded 161 enslaved Native Americans and 680 enslaved Africans. Before enslaved Indian labor started being used in New Orleans in the 1720s, tens of thousands of Indigenous People had been captured and sold elsewhere—some were sent to the French and British colonies in the Caribbean, others to plantations on the Eastern Seaboard. Usner, 12.

33. Blight, *Race and Reunion*, 5.

34. I would like to thank the anonymous *NAIS* reviewer for offering this interpretation.

35. Harjo, 43.

36. Harjo, 45.

37. Occupy Wall Street started in September 2011 in Zuccotti Park in New York City's financial district in Lower Manhattan to protest widespread economic inequality in the aftermath of the 2008 crisis. This initial occupation gave rise to the Occupy Movement in cities across the U.S. as well as globally.

38. Erdrich, Moniz, Jr, and Thunder, "Pre-Occupied." Watch the video poem on Erdrich's website: http://heiderdrich.com/video/pre-occupied/.

39. Erdrich, "Pre-Occupied," 24.

40. LeMenager, *Living Oil*, 184.

41. Erdrich, 22.

42. Furlan, *Indigenous Cities*, 141.

43. Furlan, 132.

44. Furlan, 135–137.

45. Gould and Rock, "Wakan Tipi and Indian Mounds Park," 225, 230–232.

46. Westerman and White, *Mni Sota Makoce*, 219.

47. Gould and Rock, 230.

48. Voyles, *Wastelanding*, 26.

49. "Lower Phalen Creek Project—What We Do," https://www.lowerphalen-creek.org/whatwedo.

50. Westerman and White, 5.

51. The tribe had declared retaliation against the settler government to protect their homelands from invasion. Dakota historian Waziyatawin

demonstrates that in the winter following the war, Fort Snelling functioned as a concentration camp, arguing that settlers enacted a "genocidal culture." Waziyatawin, "Colonial Calibrations," 455–461, 472.

52. Millikan, "The Great Treasure of the Fort Snelling Prison Camp," 15.

53. Erdrich, 22.

54. Erdrich, 23.

55. Brooks, "The Primacy of the Present, the Primacy of Place," 309.

56. Bernardin, "'There's a River to Consider,'"42, 52.

57. The piece uses marker, graphite, watercolor, acrylic paint, paper, and leaves on Masonite. The Milky Way Mississippi runs diagonally across the painting, with the three islands around St. Anthony Falls clearly marking the geography of downtown Minneapolis. Anderson, *Stories from St. Anthony #3*.

58. Hughes, *Weary Blues*, 33.

59. Hughes, *The Big Sea*, 54–55.

60. Hughes, *The Big Sea*, 55.

61. Bernardin, 43.

62. Erdrich, 23.

63. Harjo, 45.

64. Waziyatawin, 464.

65. Erdrich, 23.

66. Indigenous dispossession, Joanne Barker contends, is a "structural component of U.S. economics." It ranges from the defrauding of the Lenape of Manna-hata in 1626 to present modes of dispossession (including but not limited to predatory lending practices, toxic waste disposal, and mineral and oil extraction) to the refusal of Occupy Wall Street to examine its own colonial logic, which is informed by historical amnesia and the language of occupation. Barker, "Territory as Analytic," 24, 25–31.

67. Erdrich, 24.

68. Erdrich, 23–24.

69. Erdrich, 23.

70. Erdrich, 23. The line refers to the 1969 Indigenous occupation of Alcatraz and the 1973 occupation of Wounded Knee, the site of an 1890 massacre on the Lakota Pine Ridge Indian Reservation in South Dakota.

71. Hughes, *Weary Blues*, 33.

TEREZA M. SZEGHI

# Culturally Responsive Persuasion in Alexander Posey's *Fus Fixico Letters*

## Abstract

Alexander Posey (1873–1908) was a Creek humorist, journalist, editor, and poet who crafted his Fus Fixico letters to help fellow Creeks negotiate upheavals wrought by allotment, dissolution of their tribal government, and Oklahoma's impending statehood (which ultimately incorporated Indian Territory). While validating his people's varied perspectives with a culturally responsive approach to literary persuasion, Posey nudged readers toward positions he thought best for Creek cultural continuance and economic survival. The letters' dialogic structure—inclusive of diverse political perspectives—validated his people's community-oriented values and was more persuasive than prescriptive. Posey utilized four overlapping rhetorical strategies in his literary approach to political activism: *satire* and *repetition* to critique the delay of allotment deeds; *illustrative logic* to argue against U.S. assimilationism; and *appeals to civic inclusion* to protest settlers' hobbling of Indigenous Peoples' political agency and autonomy. Critical attention to Posey's use of these strategies illuminates his vision for Creek futurity as engaging with a politics of recognition while grappling with its limitations.

CREEK HUMORIST, journalist, and poet Alexander Posey (1873–1908) penned his view of the limited persuasive value of editorializing while editor of *The Indian Journal:*

> The Journal publishes few editorials and more local news items, because it is a newspaper and not an essay. Most of our readers have stored up editorials of their own. They have as many opinions on the leading questions of the day as they number individuals. Our editorials are only more "opinions." Now, in the way of facts, we can enlighten some of our readers every week, and we are sure they care more for news than for anybody's opinion—save their own.[1]

While Posey was not opposed to editorializing, as he often did so himself and championed fellow editorialists, this entry reflects his awareness of readers' fatigue over the ubiquity of opinion pieces when newspaper publication was feverish (nearly six hundred periodicals were published in Indian Territory before 1907).[2] Although no newspaper is without bias, Posey's point that newspapers should report facts and allow readers to draw their own conclusions underlies his approaches to literary activism.

In his Fus Fixico letters (fictionalized letters to the editor published serially from 1902 to 1908), Posey deployed an innovative combination of persuasive strategies, eschewing blunt statements of opinion he believed more likely to alienate than persuade. He appreciated that the Creek Nation was at a crossroads for its survival within the United States and wanted to influence fellow Creeks' political views. During Posey's lifetime, the Creek Nation and the other so-called Five Civilized Tribes faced forced dissolution of their tribal governments and allotment of their communally held lands into individually owned parcels, following the 1898 Curtis Act, which extended the 1887 Dawes Act's terms to the Five Tribes.[3] They also confronted Oklahoma's impending statehood, which combined Indian and Oklahoma Territories into one state, further eroding tribal sovereignty. This tumultuous era came after a brief period of relative stability following removal from their southeastern U.S. homelands, subsequent to the 1830 Indian Removal Act (resulting in the deaths of nearly half the Creeks) and the U.S. Civil War.[4] The Creeks had largely rebounded as a self-governing nation, adopting a new constitution in 1867.

I contribute to Posey studies by explicating four rhetorical devices he used in the letters for persuasion—each assuming a featured role in his handling of specific political issues: *satire* and *repetition* regarding allotment deeds; *illustrative logic* regarding U.S. assimilationism; and *appeals to civic inclusion* to protest settler encroachment on Indigenous Peoples' political agency. Critical attention to these techniques offers insights into the Fus Fixico letters as works of literary activism, while illuminating how Posey adapted them to changing circumstances and approached persuasion according to Creek values. This analysis also elucidates Posey's uneasy engagement with a politics of recognition: he endorsed U.S. policies he thought useful for retaining Creek lands and self-determination under pressure from colonial expansionism but confronted the self-interest and cultural myopia that undercut the settler state's willingness to meaningfully acknowledge Indigenous rights.[5] Posey consistently emphasized the importance of Creeks hashing out their own conceptions of Creek nationhood to forge their path forward. Tracing these rhetorical lines through the letters and placing them in historical context offers entry into a culturally and politically significant body of texts that can seem opaque to many outside Posey's target audience (turn-of-the-twentieth-century Indian Territory readers, especially Creeks).

I build upon Daniel Littlefield's framing of the letters for a broad audience, as well as Craig Womack's (Muskogee Creek/Cherokee) analysis of them in the context of Creek culture and history.[6] I add new dimensions to interpretations by Littlefield, Womack, and Jace Weaver (Cherokee) that view Posey's writing as advancing Creek continuance as a culturally distinct and autonomous people.[7] I argue that Posey's prioritization of his Indian Territory readership, and the tailored choices he made to influence their political beliefs rather than those of a broader U.S. audience, are critical reasons the Fus Fixico letters merit increased attention. To date, a large body of scholarship examines how late nineteenth- and early twentieth-century writers (such as Charles Eastman, Zitkala-Ša, and Sarah Winnemucca) adapted their advocacy for Indigenous rights to combat settler conceptions of Indigenous Peoples, but fewer scholars focus on Indigenous authors who wrote for their local communities. Posey's political advocacy through regional newspapers speaks to his view, detailed below, that citizenship is a *practice* performed in everyday spaces.[8]

## Creek Politics and the Fus Fixico Letters

The Fus Fixico letters were inclusive, adaptable forms of literary activism written during tumultuous times, when it was urgent to have spaces created by and for Indigenous Peoples to validate and debate multiple political perspectives. The narrator, Fus Fixico, reports conversations of Creek full-blood traditionalists regarding dramatic changes affecting their nation, along with his own perspectives. While centering characters whose politics diverge from his own, Posey created a strategic mouthpiece in the progressive "full-blood" Fus Fixico.[9]

Posey clearly believed that literature—in the form of dialogue and debate—could influence a broader audience than a didactic editorial. Rather than simply assert his arguments, he validated traditionalist perspectives while nudging Creeks to his views. As Womack suggests, Posey "is able to present a dialogue, a range of interpretations concerning what is going on in Indian Territory, rather than one monolithic narrative like the U.S. propaganda about the benefits of the dissolution of tribes and turning Native people into ordinary citizens."[10] Instead of mimicking the dominant culture's assimilationist narrative, Posey upheld communal values by depicting conversations inclusive of competing perspectives. By persuading without editorializing, Posey advanced what Mvskoke (Creek) geographer and

Indigenous methodologist Laura Harjo terms "futurity," or "the act of living out the futures we wish for in a contemporary moment, and the creation of the conditions of these futures."[11] Posey promoted futurity using two critical tools Harjo identifies for achieving it: community knowledge production and collective power.[12]

To appreciate what was at stake for the Creek Nation as Posey wrote the Fus Fixico letters, we must understand Creeks' history with allotment and acculturation to U.S. settler norms. Their experiences with allotment before removal from Georgia and Alabama in the 1830s undoubtedly shaped their responses this time. The treaty of 1832, which the Creek Nation signed under coercion by state and federal officials—and pressure from white settlement—stipulated that those remaining in Alabama would receive allotments, and those who opted for removal to Indian Territory would retain their new lands "as long as the water runs."[13] In practice, however, the U.S. government expected all Creeks to sell their allotments and move to Indian Territory. Allottees were defrauded by land speculators supported in county courts, resulting in lost land and assets.[14] Violent conflicts between Creeks and U.S. settlers in Alabama escalated into the Creek War of 1836 and led to the removal of remaining Creeks from their homelands. Once established in Indian Territory, Creeks confronted the tenuousness of their new land claims. After the U.S. Civil War, the U.S. punished Creeks who sided with the Confederacy by forcing the Nation to renegotiate treaties and cede nearly half their Indian Territory lands.[15]

Debates about how to secure Creek sovereignty at the turn of the twentieth century also were shaped by history with white settlers. The confederation of independently governed towns that traditionally comprised the Creek Nation experienced contact with whites unevenly. Lower towns in the south were closer to white settlements and engaged in more cultural and racial mixing, as well as economic exchanges, while Upper towns farther north remained resistant. One legacy was that mixed-blood members of the Creek Nation often favored so-called progressive positions (adopting elements of settler culture, for example), while full-bloods tended to resist imposed changes. These divisions influenced Posey's upbringing, politics, and writing. However, with his choice of a progressive full-blood persona, he indicated the permeability of these racialized political categories.[16]

To fairly assess Posey's position within the sociopolitical landscape of the Creek Nation, Indian Territory, and later Oklahoma, it is necessary to be mindful of contemporaneous debates about competing conceptions of Creek sovereignty. As David Chang argues, debates between competing and newly racialized political groups "in the decades following the Civil War expressed fundamental disagreement over the nature of the Creek Nation but encouraged a mutual emphasis on the centrality of Creek nationhood to the Creek future."[17] Even as factions disagreed about critical matters such as whether Creeks of African descent should enjoy full Creek citizenship rights (as required by the 1866 treaty with the U.S.), when allotment was presented to the Creek Nation and the rest of the Five Tribes in March 1894, all tribal delegates were opposed.[18] As Chang observes, though, this opposition fractured over time: "The pressures to accept allotment were enormous, however, and by 1895 a minority of Indian citizens, often of mixed heritage, reluctantly endorsed allotment—while rejecting the notion that their thinking was driven by race or economic self-interest."[19] Posey was one such mixed-blood Creek who maintained that allotment had become inevitable and the Five Tribes would fare best by taking some control of the process.[20]

Scott Lyons's conception of the "x-mark" applies here; there are no simple or pure choices for Indigenous Peoples confronting settler colonialism.

> An x-mark is a sign of consent in a context of coercion; it is the agreement one makes when there seems to be little choice in the matter. To the extent that little choice isn't quite the same thing as no choice, it signifies Indian agency. To the extent that little choice isn't exactly what is meant by the word *liberty*, it signifies the political realities of the treaty era.[21]

Lyons makes plain that ceding some measure of land and sovereignty does not amount to giving up on Indigenous Peoplehood: "An x-mark is a commitment to living in new and perhaps unfamiliar ways, yet without promising to give up one's people, values, or sense of community" (169). The Fus Fixico letters speak to the complexities of allotment and present a more accurate and nuanced understanding of Creek Nation politics than a simplistic pro/con framing. The letters' serial publication also enabled Posey to reflect his and his people's shifting opinions of a dynamic sociopolitical landscape. As Posey witnessed widespread graft and inefficiencies in allotment, for instance, he became increasingly critical of the process.

Ultimately allotment generated considerable suffering for U.S. Indigenous Peoples; their land base shrank from around 138 million to 48 million acres between 1887 and 1934.[22] Posey's endorsement of allotment, however, should be understood as a response to external impositions—an affirmation of Creek futurity in the context of limited options. The U.S. government determined Native lands would be allotted, and Posey and others believed that Creeks who did not secure their land claims would become destitute. Opposition leaders like Chitto Harjo ("Crazy Snake," leader of the conservative Snake faction) firmly resisted, with the prescient view that concession would further undermine the future viability of tribal nations.[23] Nonetheless, it is a mistake to suggest that Indigenous Peoples who favored appropriating the process to their own ends had abandoned their tribes' interests. This does not imply that they lacked any self-interested motives but does indicate their constrained choices.

Several contemporaneous regional newspapers reported Posey's work for the Dawes Commission "scouring the country" registering people for allotments.[24] Retaining Creek land in Creeks' hands, and thereby the material foundation to thrive within the U.S., was an acute concern for Posey, and reason to sign up for an allotment. There was urgency to this work, reviled though it was by some, particularly the Snakes (and some members of the Five Tribes to this day).[25] On October 19, 1905, for instance, the *Daily Ardmoreite* published "Crazy Snake Full of Talk," which records Harjo's words as Posey approached his house. Harjo asserted the continued relevance of treaties that protect Indigenous land rights before turning his ire on Posey: "I am at my own home here on my own ground and I do not wish to be disturbed by anyone. I do not try to make others listen to my views and no one has any right to tell me at my own house, in my own yard, what I should do." Posey seemed to take the exchange in stride: "Posey said that Chitto Harjo's harangue was the most eloquent Snake speech he ever listened to. 'It was a classic.'"[26] In the end, however we characterize Posey's perspective, it fit firmly within debates that defined Creek politics.[27]

Posey situated the letters within his regional context—in subject and (crucial to his persuasive aims) style. He modeled his most vocal characters, Choela and Hotgun, on real, contemporaneous Creek men. Posey made these characters credible through their Creek-English dialect, familiar to his readers, and validated distinctive aspects of Creek culture and experience.[28] As Womack argues, Posey's use of dialect "deprioritizes outsider discussion *about* Creeks in favor of dialogue within the community" and rejects assimilationism by refusing to conform to language accessible to white readers.[29] Even the wholly fictional Kono Harjo and Wolf Warrior, who express themselves mostly by grunting or spitting, represent, in Littlefield's view, "a type of individual commonly encountered in the remoter parts of the Creek Nation."[30] Womack interprets Posey's steady references to Creek oral tradition as a code that allowed him to communicate freely about politics without outsiders understanding, leading Womack to view Posey as a trickster figure who, like all tricksters—including the Creeks' Choffee/Rabbit—uses wit and cunning to defeat more formidable opponents.[31]

Posey's strategy of writing in code is significant because, while he wrote for a local audience, he also gained national attention. The letters were published throughout Territory newspapers, including the *Indian Journal* and the *Muskogee Evening Times* (both of which Posey edited at times during his publication of the letters), and sometimes made the pages of newspapers as far afield as the East Coast, although that was not his goal: "I write exclusively of the West, of home scenes and places, and fearing that my local allusions might not be appreciated elsewhere, I have never made any attempt to get a hearing in the East."[32] Posey firmly situated his writing within his tribal and geographic context. Importantly, Posey's newspaper columns worked against a long history of stereotypical representations of Indigenous Peoples as warlike or noble savages, which remained ubiquitous in the nineteenth-century press.[33] Such stereotypes were used to justify aggression against Indigenous Peoples, including theft of their lands.

Even in his regional context, Posey's readership included many white settlers, whose norms he routinely excoriated.[34] Also, during this period English language literacy favored Creeks with Western-style educations, the majority of whom were of mixed Indigenous, European, and sometimes African descent.[35] Many full-blood and/or politically conservative/traditional members of the tribe may not have read the letters firsthand but could have had the letters read to them. In any case, Posey represented their perspectives within the local press as part of the Creek Nation's public conversation.

Readers who "have stored up editorials of their own" and might not care for Posey's, could be drawn into the conversations of Choela, Hotgun, and their companions.[36] Readers could feel entertained, culturally validated, assured their concerns were shared—and, if Posey's aims were met, swayed toward his views, including that signing up for an allotment would secure their lands and cultural continuance. The letters thus engage community knowledge and collective power as tools for Creek futurity. Simultaneously, Posey paired the letters' dialogical and varied methods of persuasion with his own overt political statements (and others' reporting) published in Indian Territory newspapers as he became a notable figure throughout the region.[37]

### (Mis)Management of Allotment: Persuasion Through Satire and Repetition

During allotment, Posey dedicated considerable space in the letters to a debate echoing throughout Territory newspapers over the long wait for deeds. Posey used biting satire amplified by repetition to expose the consequences of the wait. Without deeds, allottees could not sell their lands or realize promised benefits of individual land ownership. Posey made his view of the delays clear: "The country is not going to develop until the Indians get their deeds. Delay of deeds means delay of progress."[38] While Creek Chief Pleasant Porter had public support for his efforts to add protections for Creek allottees against land grafters flooding Indian Territory before issuing deeds, Posey regarded these efforts as excuses for further delay.[39] Even after a supplemental agreement with additional protections was signed, deeds were issued far too slowly, in Posey's view, enabling corporations and non-Native settlers to seize Creek lands.

While Posey believed allotment deeds were the best defense against grafters, G. W. Grayson took a different view that Posey published as editor of the *Indian Journal,* illustrating how he valued competing perspectives and community knowledge production. Grayson, acknowledging his position was unpopular and characterized by some as "anti-progress," wrote, "You, dear editor, myself, and a possible hundred other Creeks, may wish that title would issue so that we might go into the real estate business at once; but the 13900 other Creeks and negroes who constitute our nation proper, are entering no complaints about their deeds."[40] For Grayson, these 13,900 others were going about life as usual, and only those itching to jump into real estate were anxious for deeds. Meanwhile, a competing concern Posey and others raised was that because traditional, full-blood Creeks were more likely to resist signing up for an allotment, they were disproportionately disenfranchised or assigned allotments far from their homes.

One of Posey's most utilized didactic tools was emphasizing absurdity through repetition—calling attention to the duration or frequency of an issue to amplify his point. Apparently aiming to pressure those in power to expedite allotment deeds, Posey paired his assertions about the dangers of delay, made as editor of the *Indian Journal,* with repeated illustrations in the Fus Fixico letters of its effects. In addition to his straightforward statement that delaying deeds meant delaying progress, in the letters Posey consistently countered arguments by Grayson and others that Creek traditionalists were unaffected by the wait. Like waiting itself, when it can be difficult to focus on anything except one's unfulfilled desire, the letters return repeatedly to absent deeds. Posey's use of repetition resonates with Creek oral tradition, where stories sustain their value through repeated tellings, with adaptations reflecting different speakers, audiences, and contexts.[41] Repetition also is used for comedic effect, ceremony, and underscoring important values—as well as deviations from established norms. As Womack notes, it is a stock feature of oral storytelling, used to create rhythm, tension, and draw attention to *how* a story is told, rather than simply *what* it is about.[42]

Posey deployed repetition to validate how exasperating delays felt and to illustrate what he regarded as the ridiculousness of the wait time. For example, in letter four (*Indian Journal,* December 12, 1902), Fus Fixico reflects, "Well, so I guess when I was go to the postoffice next time I get my deed for Christmas times. Choela he say he was druther had a ticket to Mexico instead of a deed, and Hotgun he says the same thing too. If Porter don't hurry up maybe they go horse back or 'foot.'"[43] Fus references conservative

Creek emigration plans to Mexico to escape allotment's impositions on traditional lifeways. In this early letter, Posey primarily uses these references comedically to advance his argument that delayed deeds may erode whatever willingness traditionalists might have to accept allotment. However, as traditional Creeks became increasingly disenfranchised through allotment and statehood, he began to see emigration as a potentially good alternative for them.[44] While Choela and Hotgun suggest that a ticket to Mexico might be preferable to a deed, Fus's proposition that his friends could become desperate enough to attempt the journey on foot paints a humorous but biting image with its implications for many Creeks' growing financial straits.

Posey amplifies the wait for allotment deeds, underscored through repetition, by presenting the chance of ever getting one as increasingly unrealistic. For instance, while Choela and Hotgun envision a ticket to Mexico as a substitute for a deed at a time when Posey viewed emigration as fanciful, Fus likens his to a Christmas present in letter seven: "Well, so I was had bad luck Christmas times. I was fly out of bed soon about daylight and look in my socks, but I was see nothing in there but big holes" (*Indian Journal*, January 2, 1903).[45] The image of Fus leaping from bed at dawn and gazing into his socks for a deed, like a present having arrived miraculously in his stocking, turns the prospect of a deed into a childish fantasy. Posey spoofs a process that should proceed as a legal transaction whereby all Creek citizens receive documentation of their land claims.

The holes Fus finds in his socks speak, facetiously, to his progressively dire financial situation, as referenced in letter three (*Indian Journal*, November 21, 1902): "I don't know what I do if I don't get my deed pretty soon. The land buyer say he can't give me but 15c for my land if them deeds don't show up. So you see I was in a bad fix for Christmas times with nothing but sour sofky to make me feel good."[46] While linking his awaited deed to Christmas frames the issue lightheartedly, the repeated references emphasize the protracted wait and its financial consequences, as well as Fus's growing disillusionment with the process. This linkage also resonates with Creek oral tradition, in which phrases and patterns of behavior are repeated to amplify character traits, plot points, and incremental knowledge production.[47] While Fus further underscores his financial precarity by noting he has only sour sofky for comfort, it is important to appreciate the cultural significance of this Creek staple food (made of corn cooked in lye water) to understand its value for Fus. Throughout the letters, sofky signifies Creek culture and comfort—as it does in Creek oral tradition, where stories like "The Origin of Corn" explain how a woman gifted corn to the people from her body and introduced sofky to household visitors.[48]

As the letters and the wait proceed, Fus turns to restrictions placed specifically on full-blood Creeks' ability to sell their allotment lands, an issue debated broadly in Territory periodicals. As he reflects in letter fourteen (*Indian Journal*, March 27, 1903): "But like I say all time, fullblood Injin was not want nothing any more but deeds, but seem like big man in Washington and big man in Creek nation was hold him down so he couldn't get it and he was had to trade it out in due bills."[49] Fus highlights power dynamics that forced full-blood Creeks to wait for the livelihood allotment proponents promised, while "big" men both near and far "hold him down." Even as Posey persistently advocates for allotment, he points to ways allotment was used not just to dismantle the Creek government but also to shift sociopolitical norms from traditional Creek conceptions of shared governance to a hierarchical model.

While some saw allotment restrictions as protective, Posey decried them as racist articulations of Indigenous identity that correlated higher blood quantum with financial incompetence. As Chang argues, allotment legally codified racialized notions of Native identity then foreign to the Creek Nation but that came to shape its internal debates about tribal citizenship and rights in subsequent decades.[50] The 1906 Five Tribes Act, for instance, "denied any 'full-blood Indian' of the Five Tribes the 'power to alienate, sell, dispose of, or encumber in any manner' any part of his or her allotment for twenty-five years (that is, until 1931). Thus, for Indians registered as 'full-bloods,' restrictions would last longer than stated in the original agreements but would also cover their entire allotment, homestead and surplus."[51]

Posey's friend and frequent interlocuter, Charles Gibson, who published his column "Gibson's Rifle Shots" in the *Indian Journal*, agreed that racism motivated allotment restrictions. In his November 11, 1904 column, Gibson argued for Indigenous Peoples' right to sell portions of their allotments:

> There is so much sympathy for the Indian that he is in danger of being smothered. This old sympathy has come too late to do the Indian any good. Sympathy is all right when it will have the desired effect. Tub fulls of sympathy will be wasted now as Mr. Indian has slipped up and is not on his feet any more, he has made too many treaties for his own good, has given up all his property, customs and rights as an Indian.[52]

For Gibson, restrictions on Indigenous Peoples' land sales were either misguided attempts to protect them or fraud masked as sympathy. He juxtaposed what he saw as false sympathy with tangible legal changes in Indigenous Peoples' social, cultural, and political status—revealing that whatever the spirit behind ostensible sympathy, it had been useless for improving Indigenous lives. As historian Cornsilk (Cherokee Nation Citizen, United Keetoowah Band) observes,

> Once the federal government began chipping away at the protection [. . .] one of the things that was detrimental to the Natives owning restricted land was that it brought them under the jurisdiction of the county court and so a county court judge could remove the restrictions or [. . .] wreak havoc with the probate or appoint guardians and all of those sorts of things that did not affect the person whose lands were not restricted. And so if I were a restricted Indian even though it appears that my land is protected by these restrictions, it really isn't because all it does is just mark me as prey for those who would try to take my land away from me.[53]

The federal erosion of protections on restricted lands Cornsilk describes began once the allotment process ended in 1907—the year before Posey's death. Even while penning the early Fus Fixico letters, though, Posey was alarmed by corporations and land grafters seizing Indigenous lands. He became more alarmed as the allotment process unfolded, as speculators bypassed restrictions.[54]

Key to Posey's public role negotiating allotment's complexities and Creek futurity was focusing his satirical lens on white settlers and U.S. policies. Reading the letters alongside other columns in regional periodicals deepens our understanding of them in relation to broader conversations about and responses to federal Indian policy. For instance, in another alignment between Gibson's and Posey's views, letter sixty-six (*Muskogee Daily Phoenix*, June 24, 1906) includes Hotgun contextualizing useless philanthropy within the history of impractical settler outreach toward Indigenous Peoples. The letter implies that Posey's support for allotment was about Indigenous self-determination and not uncritical embrace of white culture or its assimilationist mandates:

> Well, so before statehood they was too much sentiment mixed up in the Indian problem. The missionary he tell the Injin he must lay up treasures in Heaven, but didn't show 'im how to keep body an' soul together on earth and lay by for the rainy day; an' the school teacher he learn 'im how to read an' shade 'is letters when he write, but didn't teach 'im how to make two blades o' grass grow out o' one; an' the philantropist [*sic*] remind 'im o' the century o' dishonor instead o' the future individual responsibility; an' the government dish out beef an' annuity to 'im instead of a mule an' a plow. Everything like that make the Injin no count, except give jobs to government clerks.[55]

Throughout the letters, Posey satirizes settler norms forced upon Indigenous Peoples as impractical and self-serving. Hotgun amplifies their impracticality by framing Christian conversion as an effort to store "treasures in Heaven," which could include salvation but more readily evokes material possessions needed on earth to survive and thrive (and "keep body an' soul together"). Writing instruction, in turn, is not for communication but to demonstrate style, with shaded letters.

With "century o' dishonor" Hotgun references Helen Hunt Jackson's 1881 *A Century of Dishonor,* which catalogued treaties the U.S. government broke with Native tribes. For Hotgun, knowing this history imparts no tangible benefit to Indigenous Peoples, just as, in his view, religious instruction and settler-style education lack practicality. He suggests this work primarily gives white people a sense of purpose and a paycheck (e.g., jobs for government clerks). Perhaps most importantly, it undermines Native peoples' ability to meet the assimilationist imperative to thrive through individual effort, with the government allegedly sending food and payment rather than tools needed (mule and plow) to produce one's own food and revenue. That Hotgun offers these examples in a single sentence, each conjoined with "an,'" creates a rhythm resonant with oral storytelling, while underscoring the relentlessness of white intervention in Indigenous affairs. Finally, at a time when Indigenous Peoples and their resources were being counted and catalogued, and lands distributed for others' benefit, the idea of settler advocacy making the "Injin no count" carries profound implications for their standing in the United States. Hotgun's assertion of this last point contains added punch with its inclusion in a short, declarative statement following the lengthy sentence excoriating white philanthropy.

Posey's use of satire to persuade readers turns not just on settlers, but also communities within the Creek Nation. To bolster his argument for full-bloods having unrestricted land claims and agency over their affairs, for example, Posey does not depict them as financially savvy but instead satirizes settler land management ideals. This is one way the letters reflect Posey's centering of Creek perspectives and refusal to cater to settler values, even at risk of perpetuating stereotypes about Indigenous Peoples as lazy. For example, in letter eighteen, Fus Fixico recalls,

> Tookpafka Micco he say he was druther had a deed to his land than a big name in the newspaper. When I ask him what he do after he sell his land, he say he don't know, like Bob Ingersoll [an agnostic writer Posey admired]. Then he say he was let the future take care of its own self like a calf when it was get too old to suck. Guess so Tookpafka Micco was made up his mind to drink sofky and eat sour bread and be glad like a young cat with a ball a yarn before the fire place in the winter time.[56]

Tookpafka Micco asserts his right to do what he pleases with his resources, rather than making the case by detailing a strategy for profiting by his land. Through Tookpafka Micco, Posey emphasizes that willingness to embrace allotment does not equal assimilationism and that the agency Indigenous

Peoples were promised via allotment includes the right to eschew settler conceptions of industrious land use. In likening Tookpafka Micco eating and drinking merrily to a young cat playing with yarn, Fus prioritizes joy over wealth and suggests that Creeks can sever allotment from assimilationism by appropriating the process for their own ends.

Resistance to settler ideals of industriousness and wealth acquisition also can be understood as affirming Creek conceptions of prosperity and communalism. As Womack notes, "What whites and progressive Indians interpreted as laziness in the full-bloods was not laziness at all; it was a communal spirit whites did not comprehend."[57] Chief Pleasant Porter tried educating Senators touring Indian Territory prior to statehood on this point, noting that before allotment his people "always raised enough to eat, and that was all we wanted."[58] He explained that Creeks worked together and supported neighbors in need: "everything was done under the care of the people—they did everything and looked after the welfare of everything. . . . We have striven in our own way for our elevation and uplifting, and for a time it seemed that we were actually going to evolve a sort of civilization that would suit our temperament."[59] Although Porter did not mention that the Creek Nation had its own governance and educational systems prior to Europeans' arrival—perhaps finding it more strategic to focus on Creek efforts to incorporate certain settler norms—he highlighted the fact that white mania for Native lands had not, despite his people's best efforts, aided their prosperity.

In referring to the final decades of the nineteenth century as idyllic, Porter underscored Creeks' resilience when left to manage their own affairs and determine "a sort of civilization that would suit our temperament." He suggested that no one-size form of civilization fits all and that the Creek Nation's systems worked well until settlers began seizing their lands again via allotment. Posey likewise rejected white conceptions of civilization and asserted Creek rights to self-determination and cultural recognition. Posey was strategic in using the letters to *show,* rather than simply state, the validity of his critiques.

The letters' serial publication bolstered Posey's ability to persuade through repeated illustrations and his ability to adapt his argument to changing circumstances. Attention to repetition in the letters helps pinpoint where Posey's arguments shift and why. In the case of allotment, Posey was quick to protest widespread graft and land speculation in Indian Territory and call for reforms—with particular concern about predatory practices disproportionately affecting Creek full-bloods.[60] According to Littlefield,

> By summer of 1903, rumors were rife that corruption was widespread among officials of the Justice and Interior departments in Indian Territory.

The growing scandal indicated that those officials, including members of the Dawes Commission, were engaged in large-scale land speculation, particularly in the Creek Nation. The process of allotment provided opportunities for the materially ambitious to make money in real estate ventures. Unfortunately, public officials who were charged with overseeing the process found that they were not immune to the prospects, and their integrity failed in many cases.[61]

Even before restrictions were removed from Creek lands, "speculators encumbered prospective titles by advancing money to allottees in return for leases of the land."[62] Additionally, Creeks were pressured into selling deceased relatives' lands, and speculators claimed so-called surplus lands that remained after allotments were distributed to all Native peoples who signed up. Meanwhile, to retain the tribal land base, Creeks like Gibson called for allotting "surplus" lands to Creeks born after the Dawes rolls closed (when the official opportunity to register for an allotment expired).[63] Like most Creeks, Posey contended that *all* Creek lands should be allotted to Creeks.[64] In letter eleven, for instance, he endorses G. W. Grayson's argument against selling these lands.

The fact that the letters repeatedly emphasize eagerness for allotment deeds before also using repetition to call attention to corruption in the allotment process arguably adds credibility to Posey's critique. Grafting and other illicit dealings in Native lands eventually became as frequent a subject of the letters as the wait for allotment deeds had been—and Posey continued to use repetition to illustrate this new argument. Letter forty-four (*Eufaula Tribune*, April 22, 1904), for instance, presents grafters as the first settlers to arrive in Indian Territory and, due to governmental corruption, indicates they were there to stay; as Hotgun states, "Well, so the grafter he been here a long time and was a pioneer, like the Dawes Commission."[65] Posey uses repetition to stress that the implementation of allotment deviated markedly from the vision sold to tribes. The letters' repeated illustrations highlight the ubiquity of corruption and showed that the problem was more than just a few bad actors taking advantage of the process.

Posey deploys one of his most distinctive satirical techniques to protest allotment corruption and call for reforms: he coins nicknames to encapsulate individuals' shortcomings. The use of nicknames, as Womack argues, nests within Creek tradition by powerfully linking one's name and identity, while functioning as puns in the form of metonymic caricature.[66] Posey uses nicknames repeatedly, for instance, to pressure Secretary of the Interior Ethan Allen Hitchcock to investigate allotment-related corruption. Letter twenty-nine (*Muskogee Daily Phoenix*, July 17, 1903) deploys an extended metaphor of smoking out game for such investigations,

Then Hotgun he say, "Well, so I hope Secretary It's Cocked was singed they hair so the people could smell it. Maybe so that was made 'em quit running up good hands for theyselves instead a giving the Injun the chance to shuffle the deck after 'em."

And Tookpafka Micco he say, "Well, so, how they do that?"

Then Hotgun he say, "Well, so they was do it all the time, like putting 1,800 [18,000] Creek Injins on the roll when they was aint that many, counting the Seminoles too. 'Sides that they was get together and form big trust companies so they could get a corner on good times and drink Bud Wiser in they summer homes on the Grand River."[67]

Here Posey features his characters' speculation about the investigation's outcome, while educating readers about the padding of tribal rolls to appropriate Creek lands. He underscores Indigenous Peoples' exclusion from the political process—without a place at the card table. Another layer of Posey's political humor here may rest on the historical popularity of gambling among Creeks, suggesting they are being excluded from a game they played well—whether cards or, far more importantly, self-governance.[68]

Posey's repeated references to delays and graft in allotment, along with his satirizing of white politicians and U.S. settler conceptions of appropriate land management, indicate his commitment to Creek well-being. Over years of observing and participating in Indian Territory politics, Posey became a watchdog by publicizing misdeeds and advocating for his people. Having cause to mention a subject over and over in the letters, such as the wait for deeds, emphasizes its significance by force of repetition. Doing so satirically enabled Posey to sharpen his critique and draw on potent rhetorical tools, such as nicknaming. By putting characters differentially positioned in the Creek Nation in dialogue, Posey operated according to Creek communitarian values and centered community knowledge production.

## Commercialized Assimilationism: The Power of Illustrative Logic

Posey deploys a recurrent persuasive strategy in the Fus Fixico letters based on the belief that showing is better than telling. He invites readers to assess evidence themselves—while nudging them toward a particular conclusion. I call this method "illustrative logic," or simply illustration. Examining his use of illustration draws attention to one of his most consistent arguments: accepting allotment and participating in U.S. politics does not entail wholesale embrace of U.S. settler culture.

Posey is especially critical of the commercialization of the civilizing project, which is used to pressure Indigenous Peoples to buy useless things.

Consider, for instance, Hotgun's summary of Creeks' experience getting "civilized" in letter forty-three (*Muskogee Daily Phoenix*, April 17, 1904):

> Well, so like I start to say history was repeat itself. The Injin he sell his land in the old country (Alabama) and he sell his land in Injin Territory and was had a good time out here like back there in olden times. But back in old country he was live different, 'cause he was sit on a long chair like a fence rail—but he was no mugwump. Now the Injin was sit on a chair that was had fore legs and hind legs too, like a oxen, and also a cusion [*sic*] soft like moss. He was got civilized and called the old chair a bench. He wear a white shirt now and black clothes and shoes that was look like a ripe musk melon.[69]

According to Hotgun, for all the accommodations Creeks made to settler expectations, the only substantive change is that his people have far less land—and look sillier wearing allegedly refined clothing. It is difficult to make a compelling argument, for example, that sitting on a certain type of chair rather than a bench (or changing the term for the latter) transforms the sitter, which Hotgun underscores by comparing these images side by side. This illustrative logic renders assimilationism and its material expressions absurd. Hotgun parodies white conceptions of being civilized while illustrating his people's historically rooted willingness to adapt and change when it fosters their well-being.[70]

Posey's critiques of commercialized assimilationism via illustrative logic in letter forty-three appear sharper when viewed in their original publication context. This letter, which includes another vivid example of useless goods pedaled in Indian Territory as an Indigenous person is persuaded to buy a buggy that winds up "under a tree to look at like a fine painting," was printed by the *Daily Chieftain* alongside boosterism for the region based on its alleged economic success:

> While some of our people are excited over oil speculation, and many are impatient at government conditions and other hindrances, the fact remains that Vinita continues to grow and prosper. There are no empty dwellings, no business houses, and many new people are locating here.[71]

This representation of the Territory suggests that everything is vital and utilized—no empty building, and, presumably, no buggies idling under trees. Read in relation to this boosterism, Posey's parodying of settler culture and its consumerism (in the service of assimilationism) is even more striking for its commitment to Creek futurity. The lived experiences and well-being of Creeks are foregrounded, and assimilationism is exposed as predatory. While the *Daily Chieftain* article measures the region's success partially through new settlement, Posey's letter forty-three presents the intrusion of white settlers and their wares as useless impositions that leave Creeks worse off. As allotment and dissolution of tribal governments proceeded, the Five Tribes suffered economically and culturally as they lost control of their shared resources. Internal political divisions widened as tribal sovereignty, to which both progressives and conservatives were deeply committed, was dismantled.[72]

The letters abound with similarly humorous but devastating illustrations of the costs of assimilationism for Creeks, as when Fus Fixico comments in letter eighteen (*Indian Journal*, April 24, 1903) on the expectation that they Anglicize their names: "Big Man say Injin name like Sitting Bull or Tecumseh was too hard to remember and don't sound civilized like General Cussed Her or old Grand Pa Harry's Son."[73] This sentence ends a paragraph, without further comment—suggesting readers, aided by Posey's nicknaming, can discern for themselves that these Anglicized names appear more convoluted and unrefined than their Indigenous counterparts. For his Indigenous readers, of course, the deeper cultural implications of forced name changes were well known and could be invoked to strong effect without fuller explication.

Focus on the letters' illustrative logic reveals critiques of non-Native conceptions of progress and commercialized assimilation; the overt commentary of Posey's characters echoes these critiques. As if in conversation with *The Daily Chieftain*'s brand of boosterism, Fus Fixico reflects in letter eighteen,

> Well, so we hear lots a talk about big progress in Creek Nation and read about it in the newspaper before breakfast time. [. . .] But look like you don't hear nothing about fullblood Injins 'way back behind the hills that was had they sofky patch and cabin on land that was done filed on by some half-breed or maybe so white man that was had a right. We don't hear about them kind a Injin at all.[74]

Here Posey addresses omissions in the periodical press that Fus identifies, underscored with references to what Creeks hear and read about ("big progress") and what they do not (full-blood Creeks' land losses). In light of the racialized disparities in allotment, it is significant that Posey constructs Fus Fixico as a full-blood speaker of Creek-English dialect offering a corrective to dominant narratives about happenings in Indian Territory. Posey's critique is presented by someone close to the concerns he articulates and who engages in community-centered dialogue about Creek futurity and scans as a cultural insider for Creek readers.

## Appeals to Civic Inclusion

Paired with Posey's critiques of useless goods foisted on Indian Territory under the banners of civilization and progress was his advocacy for Indigenous People's agency managing their own affairs. For Posey, Creeks' equal political participation was vital to combatting injustices in allotment, self-serving white politicians, and assimilationism. The letters consistently exemplify how Creeks' appropriation of imposed changes for their own continuance is undermined by their exclusion from the political sphere. What emerges is another powerful rhetorical tool Posey used to expose disparities between U.S. ideals and the governance of Indian Territory and to identify biases within the settler state/culture that forestall its recognition of Indigenous rights.

Amid debates over Oklahoma statehood and whether Indian Territory would be incorporated within it or made a separate state, having a political voice was particularly urgent. While Posey initially mocked the prospect of separate statehood, he championed it once separate statehood seemed viable to him.[75] To advocate for separate statehood he used the letters to call out corruption in the deliberation process. For instance, as recorded in letter sixty-five (*New-Star Tribune,* March 29, 1906):

> An' Hot Gun he smoke an' go on an' say: "Well so, same way like the animals, all the politicians was hold big powwow in Washington to settle the mighty issues o' the day. Uncle Joe, the big man o' the house, was preside over the meetin', an' Oklahoma an' Injin Territory was the rabbit after the nice fruit o' statehood on the sycamore tree."[76]

Hotgun offers an outsider's perspective on political wrangling—the outcome of which will dramatically affect him—with no agency to participate. These decisions were being made far from Indian Territory, in Washington D.C., by people disconnected from those most impacted by them. Posey compares the Territories to Choffee/Rabbit and statehood to the sycamore balls he picks, based on their size, for his species to eat in perpetuity. When the balls do not fall, Rabbit nearly starves and eventually steals fruit from wiser and less opportunistic animals.[77] Here Posey's allusion to Creek oral tradition is shorthand for Creek readers, exposing the statehood process as political theater with only negative consequences for residents of the Territories. Hotgun's framing of the story with "same way like the animals" echoes similar language in this story of Rabbit's thievery, which begins, "In the beginning all the animals held a meeting," and elsewhere in Creek oral tradition, where animals collaborate on the formation of what would become the Creek world.[78] For Hotgun and other Creeks, however, the new reality being forged marginalizes their perspectives and values.

Critical to Posey's exposure of disparities between U.S. democratic values and the repeated hobbling of Indigenous political agency was his portrayal of white politicians as corrupt and incompetent. Posey frequently satirized such politicians by showing them passing through Indian Territory too quickly to make informed judgments. For example, letter twenty (*Indian Journal,* May 8, 1903), characterizes Secretary Hitchcock as follows:

> Well, so I like to know what kind a man Secretary It's Cocked is anyhow. Look like he didn't had no safety notch and couldn't stood cocked. He was change his mind every time before he get it made up good. When he do anything he acts like he was sorry and take it back after it's too late in the day. So he was had Tom Ryan change the message he was sent to Tams Big Pie and say, "Well, so I don't want no monkey business when I get off the train in Muskogee. I don't want to hear no brass band playing Dixie or big talk about statehood and things like that. So you must stay in your office and work same as a beaver instead of hanging up flags and running down to depot to see if it's train time yet; so when I come there sure enough the people won't think Ringling Brothers was in town to give a show."
>
> When I told Hotgun about it he say, "Well, so I don't see how Secretary It's Cocked catch on to anything down here if he don't get out with the boys and had a good time and get acquainted."[79]

Posey suggests that white politicians, not Indigenous Peoples, obstruct positive developments in Indian Territory. While Territory residents eagerly anticipate Hitchcock's arrival and prepare to celebrate, signaling readiness for political participation, Hitchcock refuses interaction with them, not wishing to hear "about statehood and things like that." Hitchcock imagines the peoples of Indian Territory as a circus audience rather than active participants in the political process. Yet, as Hotgun argues, familiarity with a people and place cannot be achieved by glancing at them through a window, much less does it equip one to authorize policies affecting them.[80] Simply stated, Hitchcock withholds recognition from Indian Territory's peoples on the most basic level.

Hitchcock's behavior indicates fundamental failures in U.S. relations with Indigenous Peoples by raising the question: How can politicians make sound judgments about places and peoples they know little about?[81] Noting the mandate that "Tams Big Pie" (Tams Bixby, then Dawes Commission chairman) continue working cloistered in his office rather than prepare for social engagement, Fus Fixico excoriates settler norms of industriousness as hollow and invoked performatively here by Hitchcock to shirk responsibilities that should entail substantial consultation with Indigenous Peoples. Posey's implicit argument is that Native peoples must have political agency to ensure their rights. As Fus reflects in letter eighteen, following his observations on disparities between media narratives of "big progress in Creek nation" and full-blood Creeks having their lands appropriated, "Must be the Big Man that was look out for Injin was look out for himself too much. Hotgun he say it was natural for the Big Man to do that way 'cause he was had the chance. Maybe so, Hotgun he say, that was the only law civilized man don't want to break" (*Indian Journal*, April 24, 1903).[82]

Hotgun's reflections on Hitchcock point to another rationale Posey offers for Indigenous Peoples' inclusion in the U.S. political process: basic fairness. Subjecting Indigenous Peoples to the ill-informed whims of figures like Hitchcock is blatantly unjust—rendering the need for self-determination even more urgent. As Posey underscores with his satirical renaming of Hitchcock as "It's Cocked," the secretary is erratic and dangerous, constantly changing his mind and always ready to fire but lacking a "safety notch." At the same time, the letters' characters repeatedly point to discrepancies between experiences of white people and of Native peoples regarding their right to retain their cultures while having a recognized position within the larger nation. Once more, straightforward logic animates the letters' political critiques. Hotgun argues for separate statehood on the basis that other U.S. subgroups were given their own states (e.g., Pennsylvania for Quakers and Connecticut for Yankees). He says in letter fifty-seven, "That's the way United States was founded. It was called the fundamental law. So when the Injins was want statehood congress ought to give 'em Sequoyah'" (*Muscogee Daily Phoenix,* August 27, 1905).[83] Hotgun's comedically simplistic history advances his larger claim that the system of separate states within the U.S. supports the coexistence of distinctive cultures. In his view, it makes little sense to conjoin Indian and Oklahoma Territories when "the two countries didn't had nothing in common, unless, maybe so, it was a weakness for firewater."[84]

Posey's argument for Indigenous political engagement rests on a performative conception of citizenship resonant with Creek values and U.S. democratic ideals.[85] He argued that Indigenous Peoples *become* citizens through political participation, not by having this status conferred (or imposed, as some viewed it) upon them. Referring to an upcoming vote on a draft constitution for the proposed state of Sequoyah, in letter fifty-nine Hotgun tells his friends,

> That be a big day in the winnin' a the west an', maybe so, it be set aside so it won't get mixed up with work days. After this battle a the ballots, all Injuns be constituents instead a wards a the big man at Washington. Secretary Itscocked was had to wind up his tape an' let go the scepter then an' bow to his time subjects. An' the picnic orator could climb up on the dry goods box in the shade a the scrub oaks an' talk about this great grand and glorious country!" (Letter 59, *Muskogee Daily Phoenix,* Oct. 29, 1905).[86]

The distinction Hotgun draws between being a ward of the government and a constituent is significant to Posey's larger case for Indigenous Peoples' political participation. Through Hotgun, Posey denounces U.S. paternalism, which positions Native peoples as passive and powerless. Instead, he envisions voting as foundational to achieving political equality. Hotgun represents the change in part by picturing Hitchcock relieving himself of the attire and position of a king and making way for a member of the crowd to celebrate the country in a more democratic (albeit tongue-in-cheek) fashion.

The separate statehood effort ultimately failed, and with Oklahoma statehood the Five Tribes were forced to dismantle their tribal governments and saw their political and economic standing significantly eroded. As Posey's characters turn to life in newly formed Oklahoma, they continue to highlight violations of democratic principles. Littlefield notes in framing letter sixty-six: "For the Indian citizens, who had for the most part been left out of the political process of the proposed state, the Enabling Act [the Oklahoma statehood bill] was a major social, economic, and cultural turning point. Where they would fit in the political scheme was uncertain, but Hotgun warns of the pitfalls of becoming embroiled in party politics."[87]

As the letters continue, Fus Fixico and his friends comment on their increasing marginalization and the opportunistic white politicians who manipulate Indigenous Peoples for their votes. Posey's characters make clear that U.S. citizenship (entailed by the 1887 Dawes Act when signing up for allotment, and in 1901 conferred upon all Indigenous Peoples in Indian Territory) and ostensible inclusion in a U.S. state guarantee little for Indigenous political power and socioeconomic status.[88] They expose the limitation of a politics of recognition when formal markers of belonging carry no substantive benefits and, to the contrary, target Indigenous Peoples for new forms of exploitation. In letter sixty-seven (November 25, 1906, *Muskogee Daily Phoenix*), Hotgun reflects,

> Well, so statehood was a sad thing for the Injin, but I didn't had no tears to shed over lost tribal rule, like Crazy Snake; for the new state politician was my shepherd an' I got all I want. He was tolled me off to one side an' had business with me for my local influence. He was cultivated my acquaintance for his party's sake. He was prepared the table before me in the presence o' the bartender an' hol' up two fingers an' call for a couple o' small ones. He was tell me, "Eat, drink an' be game, for, maybe so, to-morrow I want you to vote for me."[89]

Hotgun's humor turns on a decidedly grim contrast, with the notion that Creeks' losses in self-governance are counterbalanced by a new form of political engagement in which a foundational democratic instrument (voting) is co-opted by predatory politicians. Rather than being affirmed as a citizen with an equal stake in, and a valuable perspective for, shaping the direction of the newly formed state of Oklahoma, Hotgun's judgment is blunted through inebriation to manipulate his vote.

The image of plying Native peoples with liquor to swindle them of land, sovereignty, and political influence calls to mind a long and sordid history of settler dealings and resonates with similar representations in the letters—for example, in Tokpafka Micco's[90] reply to Hotgun following the assertion above:

> Well, so long time ago the white man was put his arm 'roun' the Injin's neck an' give whiskey an' big treaty medals for his lan'. But now it come to pass the white man was had ever'thing the Injin's got but his vote. So he was tolled him back in the alley, if it was in Muskogee, or to the corner saloon, if it was in Shawnee, an' set 'em up to him an' give him entertainment an' try to trade him out of it.[91]

This bleak and predatory depiction of settlers' interaction with Indigenous Peoples functions within the letters' larger narrative about the complex dilemma facing the Creek Nation: how to move forward as a flourishing, culturally distinctive people. The humor is again appropriately grim, as Tokpafka Micco validates Hotgun's portrait of Indigenous Peoples being swindled of their votes with the aid of alcohol. He compounds Hotgun's sardonic take on what Creeks exchanged for this experience by pointing to the history of settler predation, with land exchanged for whiskey and treaty medals—reducing an enduring nation-to-nation legal agreement to a comparatively fleeting moment of celebration. Hotgun and Tokpafka Micco reinforce one another to make a shared case for how Creeks are being disenfranchised in Oklahoma; in the process they also testify to the vitality of informal spaces and methods of political resistance as they socialize by the fire.

Posey did not represent white people, politics, or lifeways as meriting uncritical embrace. He signaled that any advances his people made to ensure their well-being in the face of ever-increasing pressure to give up their lands, money, and sovereignty were achieved *in spite of* U.S. settlers, not because of them. Posey's commitment to his peoples' right to political equality and continued civic engagement connected many of the letters' subjects—from allotment to statehood to freedom of cultural expression.

## Posey's Enduring Legacies

More than a century following Posey's death in 1908, his concerns about assaults on Creek self-determination and land holdings remain relevant. The letters merit critical attention not only for their literary and cultural value—and their important role in the long history of Indigenous anticolonial activism—but also for their continued significance to Indigenous Peoples' ongoing work to secure their sovereign rights. At a time when the politics of recognition arguably has become the dominant model for achieving Indigenous rights, Posey's confrontation of the settler state's limitations in meaningfully acknowledging or materially supporting Indigenous Peoples' rights to self-determination remains salient. [92] The letters offer powerful examples of how Indigenous writers adapt storytelling practices rooted in their tribal traditions to navigate existential challenges posed by settler colonialism: not by appealing to the white mainstream but to a local (in this case primarily Creek) audience.

Understanding Posey's advocacy for allotment as allied—in his view—to the interests of the Creek Nation is not to understate the devastating consequences the Curtis Act and related policies had for Creek sovereignty. Rather, consideration of Posey's writing, his support for allotment, and his criticisms of the allotment process, speaks to how Indigenous Peoples have been repeatedly but falsely assured that their futures will be secure if they concede yet more land or political autonomy. As Lyons notes regarding the land loss and poverty the Ojibwe suffered following allotment, "Such grim results are often blamed on an impoverishment of Indian life caused by the treaties and the assimilation policies, but perhaps the more urgent lesson is simply a cautionary tale about the risks of dealing with people who don't keep their word" (7). Indeed, as Posey came to understand, no sooner did allotment commence than predatory land speculators and politicians began further disenfranchising Indigenous Peoples.

The degree to which allotment and the attendant dismantling of tribal governments would work against the interests of tribal nations has gained increased scrutiny with the deciding opinion in the 2020 U.S. Supreme Court Case, McGirt v. Oklahoma, authored by Associate Justice Neil Gorsuch, and the efforts to overturn and weaken the impact of the decision since. Jimcy McGirt argued that the state of Oklahoma lacked jurisdiction to prosecute him for sex crimes because he is Seminole and the crimes he was charged with were committed within the Creek Nation's historical reservation boundaries. Oklahoma countered that the reservation no longer exists.

Gorsuch succinctly sums up the deciding position as follows, "Today we are asked whether the land these treaties promised remains an Indian reservation for purposes of federal criminal law. Because Congress has not said otherwise, we hold the government to its word."[93] As such, the Court's majority found that major crimes committed on these lands, following the 1885 Major Crimes Act, fall to the concurrent jurisdiction of the tribe and federal government—not the state of Oklahoma.[94] As Creek legal scholar Sarah Deer explains, "what the Supreme Court decision says is that our original reservation boundaries, not necessarily the land within those boundaries, but the reservation boundaries, stay the same as they did in the treaty from 1866."[95] The finding opposed Oklahoma's argument that allotment was intended to dissolve the reservation and that state claims of jurisdiction justify state rights of jurisdiction.

Gorsuch's opinion details the treaties, laws, and policies that have shaped Creek life since the removal era and documents the many ways allotment has been used to defraud them. He observes, for instance, that Oklahoma itself pointed to a long history of broken promises with Creeks to make its case that the Creek reservation ceased to exist many years ago:

> If allotment by itself won't work, Oklahoma seeks to prove disestablishment by pointing to other ways Congress intruded on the Creek's promised right to self-governance during the allotment era. It turns out there were many. For example, just a few years before the 1901 Creek Allotment Agreement, and perhaps in an effort to pressure the Tribe to the negotiating table, Congress abolished the Creeks' tribal courts and transferred all pending civil and criminal cases to the U. S. Courts of the Indian Territory.[96]

While Gorsuch notes several violations of Creek sovereignty that occurred during Posey's lifetime, he elsewhere observes that the subsequent relationship between the U.S. government and the Creek Nation has not been a simple downward trajectory for Creeks. For example, even during the allotment era, when the Creek Nation's tribal government and court system were disbanded and lands fragmented and sold off, Gorsuch underscores that "the Creek Nation retained the power to collect taxes, operate schools, legislate through tribal ordinances, and, soon, oversee the federally mandated allotment process."[97] He also accounts for the restoration of the Creek government in 1936 (per the Oklahoma Welfare Act), at which time the Creek Nation drew up a new constitution and set of bylaws."[98] What Gorsuch's opinion does not highlight (but Posey's letters do) is the sustained history of Creek insistence on their sovereign rights. Daniel Heath Justice's observation of the Cherokees is true of the Creeks and other Indigenous nations: U.S. policy can recognize but not create the sovereignty "that had *always* been embedded within the tribal nations."[99]

Posey leveraged his positions as newspaper editor and writer to negotiate the complexities of influencing politics through words and to hazard what Lyons might refer to as an "x-mark well made"—an x-mark made in the interest of Creek futurity. Much as Posey advocated Creeks' adaptations to new circumstances, he mimicked such elasticity through his publications. He could shift his position on separate statehood and register his disillusionment about the allotment process as it unfolded within the letters due to their serial nature. Whereas politicians today might be accused of lacking integrity for changing positions, Posey responded in real time to new realities (through his characters and personal statements) in a manner reflective of many readers' own experiences navigating shifting political terrains. Posey's flexibility also can be understood as reflective of the dynamism of Creek oral tradition, where stories are designed to change from one telling to the next as shaped by speaker, context, and audience.

Allied to his vision for Creek futurity, Posey deployed a powerful combination of rhetorical strategies designed to sway fellow Creeks' political views and actions: *satire* and *repetition* to amplify the length and consequences of the wait for allotment deeds; *illustrative logic* to showcase the absurdity and harm of U.S. assimilationism; and *appeals to civic inclusion* to protest settlers' hobbling of Indigenous Peoples' agency and affirm the urgency of continued Indigenous political engagement. Despite Posey's misjudgment of allotment as a path for Creek continuance and his later, more problematic, dealings in real estate, his foundational premise that adapting to new realities was the best path for his people was not a departure from Creek tradition but rooted within it.[100] On balance, Posey should be understood as an advocate for Creek continuance and an innovator in adapting literary genres to advocate for Indigenous sovereignty in ways that represent and honor the culture and competing views of his people.

**TEREZA M. SZEGHI** is professor of comparative literature and social justice at the University of Dayton. Her research focuses on Indigenous writers' use of literature to achieve social and political change. Her publications have appeared in such journals as *Aztlán, Studies in American Indian Literature, MELUS*, and *Western American Literature*.

## References

"Disregarding Restrictions: Muskogee Dealers Buying Cherokee Lands on Theory That Indian Is No Longer a Ward of the Government." *Chickasha Daily Express*, May 5, 1905.

Chang, David A. *The Color of the Land: Race, Nation, and the Politics of Landownership in Oklahoma, 1832–1929*. Chapel Hill, NC: University of North Carolina Press, 2010.

Coward, John M. *The Newspaper Indian: Native American Identity in the Press, 1820–90*. Urbana and Chicago: University of Illinois Press, 1999.

Cornsilk, David. Personal Interview, August 11, 2019.

Coulthard, Glen Sean. *Red Skin, White Masks: Rejecting the Colonial Politics of Recognition*. Minneapolis: University of Minnesota Press, 2014.

"Crazy Snake Full of Talk," *Daily Ardmoreite*, October 19, 1905.

Dagher, Veronica. "Three Questions with Scholar Sarah Deer on Empowering

Tribal Nations to Protect Native American Women," *Wall Street Journal*, July 31, 2020, https://www.wsj.com/articles/three-questions-with-scholar -sarah-deer-on-empowering-tribal-nations-to-protect-native-american -women-11596204577.

Ellis, Larry. "Rabbit and Big Man-eater: Identity Shifts and Role Reversals in a Creek Indian Trickster Tale," *Thalia: Studies in Literary Humor* 10, no. 1/2 (1998): 3—20.

Gibson, Charles. "Gibson's Rifle Shots," *Indian Journal,* November 11, 1904.

Grayson, Eli. Personal Interviews, November 11, 2019 and February 16, 2020.

Green, Michael D. *The Politics of Indian Removal: Creek Government and Society in Crisis.* Lincoln and London: University of Nebraska Press, 1982.

*Guthrie Daily Leader,* July 14, 1903.

Harjo, Laura. *Spiral to the Stars: Mvskoke Tools of Futurity.* Tucson: University of Arizona Press, 2019.

Jaimes, M. Annette. "Federal Indian Identification Policy: A Usurpation of Indigenous Sovereignty in North America." In *The State of North America: Genocide, Colonization, and Resistance,* edited by M. Annette Jaimes, 123—38. Boston: South End Press, 1992.

Justice, Daniel Heath. *Our Fire Survives the Storm: A Cherokee Literary History.* Minneapolis: University of Minneapolis Press, 2006.

Littlefield, Daniel F. Jr. *Alex Posey: Creek Poet, Journalist, and Humorist.* Lincoln: University of Nebraska Press, 1997.

———. "The Evolution of Alex Posey's Fus Fixico Persona." *Studies in American Indian Literature* 4, no. 2/3 (Summer/Fall 1992): 136—144.

Lyons, Richard Scott. *X-Marks: Native Signatures of Ascent.* Minneapolis: University of Minnesota Press, 2010.

McGirt v. Oklahoma, 591 US (2020).

Oklahoma v. Castro-Huerta, 597 US (2022)

Posey, Alexander. *The Fus Fixico Letters.* Edited by Daniel F. Littlefield Jr. and Carol A. Petty Hunter. Norman: University of Oklahoma Press, 1993.

———. *Indian Journal,* April 4, 1902.

———. *Indian Journal,* May 16, 1902.

Riley, Sam G. "Alex Posey: Creek Indian Editor/Humorist/Poet." *American Journalism* 1, no.2 (1984): 67—76.

Swanton, John. *Myths and Tales of the Southeastern Indians.* Washington D.C.: Smithsonian Institution Bureau of American Ethnology Bulletin. U.S. Government Printing Office, 1929.

Spires, Derrick. *The Practice of Citizenship: Black Politics and Print Culture in the Early United States.* Philadelphia: University of Pennsylvania Press, 2019.

"The Sweet Singer of the Creeks," *The Brooklyn Daily Eagle,* December 2, 1900.

Szeghi, Tereza. "'The Injin is civilized and aint extinct no more than a rabbit': Transformation and Transnationalism in Alexander Posey's Fus Fixico Letters." *Studies in American Indian Literatures* 21, no. 3 (2009): 1—35.

Weaver, Jace. *That the People Might Live: Native American Literatures and Native American Community.* Oxford: Oxford University Press, 1997.

Womack, Craig. "Alexander Posey's Nature Journals: A Further Argument for

Tribally Specific Aesthetics." *Studies in American Indian Literature* 13, no. 2/3 (Summer/Fall 2001): 49–66.

———. *Red on Red: Native American Literary Separatism.* Minneapolis: University of Minnesota Press, 1999.

Zissu, Erik. *Blood Matters: The Five Civilized Tribes and the Search for Unity in the Twentieth Century.* New York: Routledge, 2001.

## Notes

1. Posey, *The Indian Journal,* April 4, 1902.

2. Riley, "Alex Posey," 67.

3. The Creek, Cherokee, Choctaw, Chickasaw, and Seminole tribes were labeled the "Five Civilized Tribes" due to adoption of some aspects of settler culture (including educational methods, dress, governance, and slavery) in hopes of proving their equality to settlers and securing their rights in the newly formed United States.

4. Harjo, *Spiral to the Stars,* 67.

5. I use "politics of recognition" to refer to advocacy for laws and policies within the settler state that affirm Indigenous nationhood and rights. Although the form recognition takes varies, as Glen Sean Coulthard explains, "most call for the delegation of land, capital, and political power from the state to Indigenous communities through a combination of land claim settlements, economic development initiatives, and self-government agreements." As Coulthard argues, however, the settler state's prioritization of its own interests undercuts the impact of such recognition for Indigenous communities, and too often reinforces colonial power structures. Coulthard, *Red Skin, White Masks,* 3.

6. See Littlefield, *Alex Posey,* and "Evolution of Alex Posey's Fus Fixico Persona"; Posey, *Fus Fixico Letters* (edited by Littlefield and Petty Hunter); and Womack, *Red on Red.*

7. Weaver, for instance, categorizes Posey as a "communitist" writer (conjoining "community" and "activism"). Communitist literature demonstrates "a proactive commitment to Native community." Weaver, *That the People Might Live,* xiii.

8. Similarly, Derrick Spires addresses Black print culture as an enactment of citizenship through which citizenship itself was forged and (re)defined, focusing on texts targeting a Black audience. Spires views citizenship as relational and developed not just through practices like voting, but also via informal interactions between community members. Spires, *The Practice of Citizenship.*

9. Posey's politics are more complex than the term "progressive" suggests (as are the views of those labeled "conservatives" or "traditionalists"). Still, I find "progressive" to be the most fitting shorthand for his politics relative to contemporaneous Creek political factions—particularly as he consistently differentiated his views from those he termed "pull-back Indians" who resisted allotment and other changes imposed on Creeks. This terminology also is consistent with most scholarship about the Creek Nation during this era. Likewise,

using blood quantum to measure Indigenous identity is a problematic colonialist construction formalized during the Dawes era to determine land rights and allotment restrictions. Nonetheless, blood quantum became a salient cultural and political identifier within the Creek Nation during this time as various factions navigated unprecedented impositions on their lifeways—as reflected in the Fus Fixico letters and scholarship on this period in Creek history.

10. Womack, *Red on Red*, 153.

11. I build here on Littlefield's argument about Posey's aim to persuade without editorializing ("The Evolution of Alex Posey's Fus Fixico Persona," 137). Harjo, *Spiral*, 5.

12. Harjo, *Spiral*, 45.

13. Per the 1826 Treaty of Washington, Creeks had ceded most of their Georgia lands (Green, *The Politics of Indian Removal*, 171).

14. Green, *Politics of Indian Removal*, 183.

15. See Zissu, *Blood Matters*, 111, n.3. Note also that Creeks who remained loyal to the Union were promised payments that were slow to come (Womack, *Red on Red*, 151).

16. As Daniel Heath Justice argues, "The terms *fullblood, mixedblood, traditional,* and *progressive* are often used as absolute terms, in that fullbloods are seen as being traditional and mixedbloods are viewed as assimilated or acculturated. Such absolutes are rarely accurate. People of all quanta (a concept descended primarily from the intersections of political and scientific racism of the nineteenth) have stood on all points of the cultural spectrum" (Justice, *Our Fire Survives*, xv.

17. Chang, *Color of the Land*, 41.

18. Chang, *Color of the Land*, 85.

19. Chang, *Color of the Land*, 88.

20. Chang, *Color of the Land*, 88.

21. Lyons. *X-Marks*, 1.

22. Jaimes. "Federal Indian Identification Policy," 126.

23. As Womack notes, "the Snakes continued to hold their own Creek government at Hickory Grounds and send delegations to Washington to argue the validity of the treaty of 1832, even though the United States did not recognize their government. The Snakes continued this resistance until the 1930s, when the United States again recognized Creek government" (*Red on Red*, 146).

24. See Chickasha Daily Express, "Disregarding Restrictions: Muskogee Dealers Buying Cherokee Lands on Theory That Indian Is No Longer a Ward of the Government," May 5, 1905.

25. David Cornsilk (Cherokee Nation citizen, United Keetoowah Band) and Eli Grayson (Muscogee), for example, view Posey as among the acculturated Creeks who embraced allotment for personal gain (personal comm.). I argue, however, that Posey's writings suggest he also viewed proactive appropriation of allotment as in the tribe's interest.

26. "Crazy Snake Full of Talk," *Daily Ardmoreite*, October 19, 1905.

27. See Womack, *Red on Red*, 141.

28. Littlefield, "Introduction," 35.

29. Womack, "Alexander Posey's Nature Journals," 51. See also Womack, *Red on Red,* 135.

30. Littlefield., "Introduction" to *The Fus Fixico Letters,* 35.

31. Womack, *Red on Red,*151, 152—153, 155.

32. Posey was editor of the *Indian Journal* from 1902 to the fall of 1903, when he sold the paper to become city editor of the *Muskogee Evening Times.* He left the latter role in spring 1904 to work for the Dawes Commission. During the last few weeks of his life, in 1908, he resumed editorship of the *Indian Journal.* See Littlefield, "Introduction," 41. Editors and readers distant from Indian Territory were intrigued by Posey, the first Indigenous humorist to gain national attention, but he repeatedly turned down opportunities to write for national papers. "The Sweet Singer of the Creeks," *The Brooklyn Daily Eagle,* December 2, 1900.

33. Coward, *The Newspaper Indian,* 5—6.

34. Zissu asserts that by 1890 white settlers outnumbered Indigenous Peoples two-to-one, *Blood Matters,* 17. However, Eli Grayson argues such a ratio would not have been possible until 1895, but that by 1898 it was closer to ten-to-one (Personal Interview, February 16, 2020).

35. Eli Grayson, Personal Interview, November 11, 2019.

36. Posey, *Indian Journal,* April 4, 1902

37. The July 14, 1903 edition of *The Guthrie Daily Leader,* for instance, reports: "Alexander Posey caused a laugh at Eufaula by saying that 'what the gander legged dudes in Washington who presume to run our affairs need is hickory poles instead of twine strings for backbones."

38. Posey, *Indian Journal,* May 16, 1902.

39. Littlefield, "Introduction," 51.

40. Grayson, *Indian Journal,* June 27 and July 11, 1902.

41. A conversation Womack records in *Red on Red* with Creek elder Linda Alexander, for example, includes an instructive discussion of factors that may have shaped her father's different iterations of the story of how turtle got its mottled shell—including the length of the story he was inclined to tell and ways particular audiences might react (79).

42. See Womack, *Red on Red,* 88—89, for discussion of repetition in the Creek oral tradition, 51—101 for a detailed account of Creek oral tradition more broadly, and 131—172 for Posey's adaptations of traditional Creek stories. For more on Creek storytelling, see also: Harjo, *Spiral;* Ellis, "Rabbit and Big Man Eater"; and Swanton, *Myths and Legends.* Note, however, potential cultural biases in Swanton's translations (Womack, *Red on Red,* 94).

43. Posey, *Letters,* 58.

44. References to emigration and their strategic function in the letters are examined in my 2009 article, "Transformation and Transnationalism in Alexander Posey's Fus Fixico Letters."

45. Posey, *Letters,* 63.

46. Posey, *Letters,* 56.

47. In "The Tasks of Rabbit," for example, in a quest for wisdom Rabbit is given a series of tasks, each involving bringing another animal to the master.

Accomplishing all, with his characteristic trickery, the master determines he has nothing to teach Rabbit. "The Tasks of Rabbit," recorded in Swanton, *Myths and Tales of the Southeastern Indians*, 58−59.

48. "The Origin of Corn," recorded in Swanton, *Myths and Legends*, 9−10.

49. Posey, *Letters*, 78.

50. Chang, *Color of the Land*, 93  95, 117.

51. Chang, *Color of the Land*, 118.

52. Gibson, "Gibson's Rifle Shots" (*Indian Journal*, November 11, 1904).

53. Cornsilk, Personal Interview, August 11, 2019.

54. See, for example, "Disregarding Restrictions: Muskogee Dealers Buying Cherokee Lands On Theory That Indian Is No Longer A Ward Of The Government" (*Chickasha Daily Express*, May 5, 1905), which discusses how the Supreme Court decision *Matter of Heff* (197 U.S. 488, 1905), deeming Indigenous allottees no longer government wards, gave land buyers a flimsy rationale for bypassing restrictions.

55. Posey, *Letters*, 248.

56. Posey, *Letters*, 88−89.

57. See Womack for a more extensive discussion of laziness in the letters—what he views as a partially stereotypical depiction of full-blood Creeks that also "reveals a spirit of resistance to white encroachment and progressivism" (*Red on Red*, 162).

58. Quoted in Zissu, *Blood Matters*, 9.

59. Quoted in Zissu, *Blood Matters*, 9.

60. See, for instance, letters thirty-one and thirty-two (April 28, 1903 and September 11, 1903, respectively, *Indian Journal*) for discussion of and skepticism toward investigations into corruption in the allotment process. Letter twelve (*Indian Journal*, March 6, 1903) offers one of several suggestions in the letters that the process is designed to benefit mixed-blood progressive Creeks and disenfranchise conservative full-bloods.

61. Littlefield, *Letters*, 119.

62. Littlefield, *Alex Posey*, 174.

63. Littlefield, *Alex Posey*, 173−175.

64. As Littlefield notes, "An issue on which most Creeks agreed was that all Creek land should be allotted to Creeks and none reserved for sale to outsiders" (*Letters*, 70−71).

65. Posey, *Letters*, 167.

66. Womack notes that Creek oral tradition contains numerous stories centering around puns and that Native peoples commonly use nicknames to encapsulate (and poke fun at) notable aspects of a person's character, *Red on Red*, 157.

67. Posey, *Letters*, 121.

68. See Ellis, "Rabbit and Big Man-eater," 10.

69. Posey, *Letters*, 165.

70. See Womack, *Red on Red*, 30−31.

71. *Daily Chieftain*, D.M. Marrs, editor, April 18, 1904.

72. See Zissu, *Blood Matters*, 9−21.

73. Posey, *Letters,* 87

74. Posey, *Letters,* 88.

75. Littlefield, *Alex Posey,* 150–153.

76. Posey, *Letters,* 246.

77. "Why the Rabbit Steals," recorded in Swanton, *Myths and Tales,* 61.

78. "Why the Rabbit Steals," recorded in Swanton, *Myths and Tales,* 61; "How Day and Night Were Divided," for example, begins with, "The animals held a meeting" before detailing how to determine the distribution of hours between night and day (recorded in *Myths and Tales,* 2).

79. Posey, *Letters,* 93.

80. This critique of white politicians creating policy for Indian Territory from a distance also was offered by other Indian Territory newspaper writers. For example, "O, Mr. Dawes" (*Indian Journal,* January 4, 1901), notes that Henry Dawes "has not seen the borders of the Indian Territory for years" and "has not done a lick of work on the [Dawes/allotment] commission in so long that has name has become a joke in the Five Tribes" despite continuing to draw a salary.

81. Notably, Posey castigates President Theodore Roosevelt for similar behavior, as in letter sixteen (*Indian Journal,* April 10, 1902), wherein "President Rooster Feather" flies through Indian Territory so quickly that people "see him go by before they could get they mouth open" (Posey, *Letters,* 82–83).

82. Posey, *Letters,* 88.

83. Posey, *Letters,* 219.

84. Posey, *Letters,* 219.

85. An excellent example of the participatory nature of traditional Creek governance is the practice of voting with one's body by standing next to one's preferred nominee. When a secret ballot was adopted with the 1867 Creek constitution, Creek traditionalists revolted in the 1871 Sands Rebellion (Womack, *Red on Red,* 36).

86. Posey, *Letters,* 227.

87. Littlefield, *Letters,* 247.

88. See Chang, *Color of the Land,* 98–99.

89. Posey, *Letters,* 251–252.

90. Posey's spelling varies between "Tookpafka Micco" and "Tokpafka Micco." I follow Posey's lead in my spelling, dependent on the letter under discussion.

91. Posey, *Letters,* 252.

92. See Coulthard, *Red Skin, White Masks,* 2.

93. *McGirt v. Oklahoma* 591 U.S. 1 (2020).

94. Oklahoma's efforts to weaken the impact of the *McGirt v. Oklahoma* decision include its filing of *Oklahoma v. Castro-Huerta.* The U.S. Supreme Court ruled in favor of Oklahoma (597 U.S., 2022), granting the state jurisdiction on tribal lands in cases where non-Native peoples commit crimes against Native peoples.

95. Quoted in Dagher, "Three Questions with Scholar Sarah Deer."

96. *McGirt v. Oklahoma* 591 U.S. 13 (2020).

97. *McGirt v. Oklahoma* 591 U.S. 14 (2020).

98. *McGirt v. Oklahoma* 591 U.S. 15–16 (2020). For more on the Oklahoma Welfare Act, See Harjo, *Spiral*, 9. Note, however, that the Bureau of Indians Affairs continued appointing the Creeks' Chief at various points until 1970 (Womack, *Red on Red,* 39–40).

99. Justice, *Our Fire Survives,* 22.

100. For Womack, "Reading Posey's life as a trickster narrative goes a long way in trying to make sense of his contradictory actions—I mean here his real estate dealings and drowning shortly thereafter—since Rabbit seeks first and foremost to satiate his own needs, often falling victim to his own greediness but also sometimes bringing about cultural transformation in spite of his avarice and victimizations" (*Red on Red,* 155). Womack thus accounts for the most troubling aspects of Posey's biography in ways that nonetheless reinforce Posey's position within the Creek community.

PHINEAS KELLY *and* CHRIS CASKEY RUSSELL

# Northern Arapaho Language Revitalization with Virtual Reality

## Abstract

In cooperation with elders of the Northern Arapaho Language and Culture Commission (NALCC), a language revitalization project using virtual reality is being developed, supported by a National Science Foundation grant. The origins of the project are explored, underlying methodologies examined, as well as the important role that the elders of the Northern Arapaho Language and Culture Commission play in guiding the goals of the grant: (a) exploring the potentials of virtual reality in language revitalization; (b) documenting spoken Arapaho language with an emphasis on hunting and animal migration stories and songs related to place names on the Wind River Indian Reservation and other locations in Wyoming and Colorado; and (c) developing virtual reality curricula units for Wind River Indian reservation K—12 schools. Difficulties in conducting research during the covid19 pandemic, especially with Indigenous communities that have been hit hard by the virus, impacted our methodology and project process. This project seeks to provide a blueprint for other scholars interested in working with tribes and grant agencies in using VR in language revitalization. The project engages the questions if and how VR and subsequent technologies can be used as decolonial tools to help reverse language loss and promote culture.

IN EARLY SEPTEMBER OF 2019, we climbed atop a stone monolith in the southeastern Wyoming region of the United States. The University of Wyoming (UW) archaeologist who brought us to the location named it the "Fortress." The Fortress holds no Indigenous name within living memory even though it had been heavily inhabited by many Indigenous groups for millennia until the removals of Native Americans from the area in the 1870s and 1880s.

We visited the Fortress at the request of Nii'eihii Neecee, Northern Arapaho culture bearer and leader of the Northern Arapaho Language and Culture Commission (NALCC) to document this land for the tribe. The NALCC is a group of elders (usually eight members with a chair) whose first language is Northern Arapaho.[1] The NALCC was created in the 1980s to promote language and culture revitalization; the Northern Arapaho Tribal/Business Council bylaws granted NALCC authority to determine language and culture curricula in reservation schools. The NALCC is seen by the Northern Arapaho tribe as the main cultural authority on the reservation.

The grounds around the Fortress are studded with thousands of rock flakes of all colors chipped off atlatl projectiles and arrow points. Flakes of dark red, yellow, and greenish-blue stand out against the sage and sandstone that dominates the area. Numerous bone flakes (bison, antelope, and deer) and fire-cracked stones from ancient hearths also crowd the area. A human-made earthen ramp runs up to the base of the Fortress, and ancient hand and foot holds carved into the stony sides give access to the top. A hollow area atop the Fortress that could hold several dozen people comfortably provides perfect shelter from the wind. The top and base contain many indentations for fires and thousands of stone and bone chips as well as pottery fragments (prehistoric pottery, the archaeologist tells us). Above the sheltered hollow, on the very top of the Fortress, dozens of human-carved holes pock the surface. The archaeologist tells us these holes may have stored maize as well as water.

The only nearby water source lies one and a half miles from the Fortress: a river named after the ranch family who owns the land.[2] We hiked there with the archeologist. Like the Fortress, the Indigenous name for this river and surrounding area is not known within living memory though the Northern Arapaho have recently renamed the area leading to the river the "Buffalo Roads." Going down the small ridge to the river are deep veinlike channels worn through the lithified clay and into the bedrock: evidence of millions of migrating buffalo following one another for thousands of years, each hoof step collecting and carrying away small bits of clay and stone.

No buffalo have been through the area since the 1870s. The Arapaho were removed around the same time, shortly after the 1864 Sand Creek Massacre.[3] By 1890, the buffalo were gone and the remaining Northern Arapaho were forced onto the Wind River Reservation in central Wyoming. The entirety of the traditional Arapaho homeland fell into governmental or private nonnative hands. The Fortress sits on a private cattle ranch owned, we were told, by the same family since the 1920s. Hundreds of thousands of bison bones and teeth remain. We found them in exposed cuts three, four, even five feet below the topsoil. Indigenous People hunted and harvested countless buffalo over the centuries here. The archaeologist told us numerous tipi rings spot the ridges and plateaus beyond the Buffalo Roads. Apparently, large villages once surrounded these roads.

We came here to record the Buffalo Roads in 3D 360-degree, panoramic photography, video, and spatial audio to incorporate into National Science Foundation (NSF)–funded virtual reality (VR) project we are creating with the 3D Visualization Center (also known as the 3D Cave) at the University of Wyoming. We will add stories of buffalo migration and buffalo hunting in the Northern Arapaho language to the 360-degree photography, video, and spatial audio in order to create a Northern Arapaho language acquisition tool. The tool will be gifted to language teachers on the Wind River Reservation to use in their Northern Arapaho language and culture classes. For this project there were three main goals: to explore the potential of virtual reality in language revitalization; to document spoken Arapaho language with an emphasis on hunting and animal migration stories and songs related to place names on the Wind River Indian Reservation and other locations in Wyoming and Colorado; and to develop virtual reality curricula for Wind River Indian Reservation K–12 schools.

As far as we know, the Northern Arapaho have been back to the Fortress and Buffalo Roads only once since their removal, when more than twenty years ago a small group of elders including Nii'eihii Neecee were allowed on the land to bury human remains that were exposed by erosion from the shifting river. We hope that VR can bring the Buffalo Roads back to the Northern Arapaho people and let them experience, at least virtually and in their own language, this now off-limits area of their traditional homeland.[4]

There were, without a doubt, ancient Arapaho names for the Buffalo Roads and the Fortress, but none of the remaining Northern Arapaho speakers can recall them. Indigenous languages imbue landscape with meaning and Indigenous place names provide contemporary Indigenous People with connection to their ancestors' lands. Like the Arapaho themselves, all their names have been removed. The entire area is now blandly called a *ranch*.

## Part I: Finding the Buffalo Roads

The seeds for the Buffalo VR project were planted in the fall of 2016. The University of Wyoming president greenlighted its American Indian Studies program to proceed with a week-long summer high school institute to bring twenty-five high-school-age Indigenous youth to campus in the summer of 2017. The students were housed in dorms, interacted with faculty and administrators in every college, got to know on-campus student resources and activities, and spent a few days in the mountains surrounding the university.

Dr. Phineas Kelly, now a postdoctoral researcher at the University of Wyoming, asked Dr. Christopher Russell, the director of American Indian Studies (AIS) at the University of Wyoming, if the program would be interested in collaborating on a mobile, place-based language application for the Northern Arapaho language—since the university was located on traditional Arapaho territory and the American Indian Studies program had close ties to, and a history of collaborating with, the Northern Arapaho tribe and the NALCC. The mobile app would be a game where users would follow a gamified storyline around the university's campus, learning Northern Arapaho language and stories as they leveled up in the game. Dr. Russell and Robyn Lopez, the Arapaho language instructor for AIS, advised Phineas to take the idea to the NALCC and introduced Phineas to Wayne C'Hair, Northern Arapaho elder, language instructor, and member of the NALCC. After a year of collaborative development with funding from AIS the Arapaho Vision Quest Augmented Reality Mobile Place-Based Arapaho Language and Culture Learning Application was formally launched on the first day of the summer institute. Two dozen American Indian high school students and a few elders spent hours walking around the university's campus playing the game on iPhones and iPads. The students often asked the elders for correct pronunciations, or if the elders knew a particular word or story. When it was over, the authors asked an elder Northern Arapaho speaker and member of the NALCC what he thought of the language app. The elder replied, "We must fight fire with fire." This initial collaboration with members of the NALCC led to a deeper partnership from which the virtual reality elicitation process, methods, and our NSF Documenting Endangered Languages grant grew.

## The Arapaho Language

The fire the elder was referring to was, of course, the destruction and loss of his Native language. After the discovery of gold near Denver in 1858, white settlers inundated the front range of Colorado, violently displacing the Arapaho tribe. The Sand Creek Massacre of 1864 is perhaps the most infamous (but not the only) example of violence against the Northern Arapaho during this era. After the Sand Creek Massacre, the tribe was split into two groups. One portion headed south to Indian Territory in Oklahoma. The other group, now known as the Northern Arapaho, decided to stay in their traditional territory, which included the southeastern portion of Wyoming and the eastern portion of Colorado from the North Platte River down to the Arkansas River, as well as large swaths of western Kansas and Nebraska. The Northern Arapaho faced constant violence from settlers and soldiers. Northern Arapaho stories from this time recall a never-ending upheaval of their lives in what remained of their traditional lands: battling disease and starvation, fighting settlers, and fleeing from the U.S. Cavalry. Ultimately, they were forced onto the Wind River Indian Reservation in 1878—a reservation that housed their traditional enemy: the Eastern Shoshone. The U.S. government promised the Northern Arapaho their own reservation, but that promise was never fulfilled.

While removal to the reservation put the Northern Arapaho out of imminent physical danger, it signaled the beginning of the destruction of their language. American Indian boarding schools, the dominance of English as the primary mode of instruction in K−12 education on the reservation, and the seemingly inexorable influence of western media and culture have all contributed to the current state of danger for the Arapaho language.

Like the tribe, the language diverged after the Sand Creek Massacre. The Northern Arapaho dialect of the Arapaho language is now critically endangered and spoken primarily on the Wind River Indian Reservation in the state of Wyoming. The most recent estimates indicate that of the total population of 5,943 fewer than 100 people actively speak the language; none of the fluent speakers are younger than 60. The Southern Arapaho dialect is spoken by a mere handful of elders, all approximately 80 years of age or older in western Oklahoma.[5] Like many Indigenous Peoples worldwide, the Arapaho are in danger of losing all first-language speakers within the next twenty years.

To make the situation more difficult, Arapaho is a polysynthetic and agglutinating language, meaning it condenses a large amount of information into long, complex verbs. These verbs often take a sentence or more to express in other languages, which makes polysynthetic languages like Arapaho particularly difficult and time-consuming as a second language to learn for English speakers. The Northern Arapaho are deeply aware of the challenges faced by their language and have long been engaged in many efforts to maintain it, producing both recorded (audio and visual) and written documentation as well as the development of a variety of language teaching curricula. With the rise of the internet, the Northern Arapaho have also been quite willing to embrace technology such as the Arapaho Vision Quest app as one tool of many to help reverse the loss of their language.

### From Mobile App to VR

After learning that the Arapaho Vision Quest app was well received by the Northern Arapaho elders and Indigenous students involved in the summer high school institute, we discussed the potential of creating a similar language application using virtual reality with members of the NALCC. The 3D Cave at the University of Wyoming has the ability to create VR programs. We could imagine a fully immersive 3D virtual environment where language and important landscape could be combined with stories from oral tradition for a fully immersive linguistic experience. We received a seed grant from the University of Wyoming in 2018 to pursue the project and worked with the 3D Cave to create a prototype VR Northern Arapaho language application. We recorded in 360-degree video an Arapaho tipi filled with traditional objects such as a backrest, clothes, bow, arrow holders, hide scrapers, and a buffalo robe. We then recorded in 360-degree video various locations within Vedauwoo, Wyoming, using a drone to navigate between locations. Vedauwoo is a dramatic landscape full of forest and rock formations in the mountains above Laramie. The Arapaho still hold Vedauwoo sacred even though they have been dispossessed of the area, and it is now a state park. The name Vedauwoo itself comes from the Arapaho word *bito'o'wu,* which means *earth* or *earthborn.* With the help of Nii'eihii Neecee, we recorded a song and story in Northern Arapaho from oral tradition about Vedauwoo. We placed the tipi, virtually, in Vedauwoo and combined that scenery with the song and story. With the Vedauwoo VR prototype ready, we were invited to demonstrate the app at an official meeting of the Northern Arapaho Language and Culture Commission (NALCC).[6]

We traveled to the Wind River Reservation with the Vedauwoo VR language prototype and VR gear; members of the NALCC donned the VR helmets and virtually stepped into the tipi. With the aid of a handheld VR pointer, the elders clicked on icons on the tipi walls and navigated around several landscapes in Vedauwoo while listening to the song and story in Northern Arapaho. They enjoyed the immersive experience and saw the potential for such applications in aiding language and cultural revitalization. We formally asked the NALCC for their support for an NSF grant application dedicated to making similar VR applications for a larger number of traditional landscapes. With their guidance, the creation of interactive VR language applications for use in Northern Arapaho language and culture classes on the reservation and at our university was proposed. NALCC members test out these language applications at all stages of development and have the final say regarding any stories, songs, and translations used.[7] At the end of the project, everything—VR applications, computers, VR equipment—will be donated to any school on or around the reservation that is interested; moreover, Northern Arapaho students at our university will be trained to implement a VR curriculum in those schools.

Nearly every elder stated that their children and grandchildren were always playing video games; they loved the idea of using that technology to teach and reconnect young people with *their* language.[8] The NALCC agreed to write a letter of support for an NSF grant application. We submitted the grant in November 2018. After much back and forth with the NSF-DEL

(Documenting Endangered Languages) director, the grant was awarded in August 2019, with three- and one-half years to complete the project. NALCC's support was and is critical for the project; NSF would not have awarded the grant were it not for the NALCC.

One major concern we shared was that though we are members of Indigenous communities, we are not members of the Northern Arapaho tribe. We did not want to collect stories or songs that are used in ceremony, especially those that are integral to the sun dance, nor did we want to collect stories or songs that are the personal property of bands or clans. The NALCC elders solved this problem. The elders told traditional stories about how the Arapaho hunted the Medicine Bow National Forest and the areas around southeastern Wyoming. The NALCC members described the area from the Snowy Range and Elk Mountain down to Blackhall Mountain in the Sierra Madre as a prime Arapaho hunting area. According to NALCC, the area north of Walden, Colorado, was called "the Door" in Arapaho due to the large concentration of animals that migrated through the corridor between Blackhall Mountain and the Snowy Range. The Arapaho would camp along Elk Mountain, which is called Wind Break or Tipi-liner in their language, and hunt those migrations. The town of Hanna near Elk Mountain means "through here" or "be here" in Arapaho and refers to those vast migrations of animals as well as the meeting of Arapaho bands during hunting season.

The stories clarified the project's focus: stories of hunting, animal migrations, and traditional subsistence methods surrounding hunting. These stories are relatively safe to collect—the NALCC assured us that such stories do not violate tribal custom. Also, many young Northern Arapaho love to hunt. The NALCC thought these stories would be interesting and inspiring to their youth.

The NALCC dictated the locations we should record. During several meetings on the reservation with the NALCC they selected appropriate locations for our project, five major locations they wanted to record so that they could put stories to them: (1) Thunder Pass, Colorado; (2) Elk Mountain, Wyoming; (3) the Buffalo Roads in southeastern Wyoming; (4) Estes Park, Colorado; and (5) the area around the powwow grounds on Wind River Reservation. The first four locations are part of the traditional Arapaho homeland. Thunder Pass and Estes Park are of special religious importance to the Arapaho and are areas from which the Arapaho were violently removed. The fifth location is part of the current Northern Arapaho homeland on Wind River Indian Reservation.

With the locations of the grant determined, we turned our attention to the technology itself: drones, 360 cameras, and VR. Given the colonial history and colonizing enterprise of technologies such as cameras, audio/video recorders, and the very fact of research on Indigenous communities, how could we be sure that we were using these technologies in a decolonizing fashion? Were our methodologies based in decolonial strategies?

## Part II: Decolonizing Virtual Reality Technologies

VR and its attendant technologies are comparatively new tools of practice-based research inquiry and the critical discussions surrounding the use of VR in research are burgeoning. Of particular interest to the field of Indigenous studies is whether or not these technologies can be used as tools of decolonization. Regardless of the intention behind their use, do they represent yet more sophisticated repackaged tools of colonization to extract and appropriate Indigenous knowledge? Do they replicate what Linda Tuhawai Smith noted regarding the dual function of older research tools? "The instruments or technologies of research were also instruments of knowledge and instruments for legitimating various colonial practices."[9]

We believe the aims and intention motivating the use of VR are of utmost importance. We have been circumspect in our aims and intentions for using VR to aid in Indigenous language revitalization. NALCC controls the subjects of data collection (sites and stories) and the data itself: how it is collected, where it is stored, and ultimately if it is used as part of the VR language revitalization curriculum to be created from the data. As Smith states, "Decolonization . . . does not mean and has not meant a total rejection of all theory or research or Western knowledge. Rather, it is about centering our concerns and world views and then coming to know and understand theory from our own perspectives and our own purposes."[10] The directional aspect of our project is important as well: it does not extract data from an Indigenous community and distribute it to the non-Native world. The team collects data from the traditional Northern Arapaho homeland (now no longer part of their territory) and brings it back to the Northern Arapaho on their current homeland—the Wind River Reservation.

One of the aims of the project is to discover if Indigenous ontology and language can be revitalized by reconnecting Indigenous People to their lands with VR applications. Can these technologies be tools to anchor Indigenous knowledge and language to the lands they now call home and—just as importantly—to the lands that have been and continue to be stolen from them? Today everything about land—from directions to and from a place, names, and detailed information—is served up in seconds on a smartphone in non-Indigenous languages. For Indigenous People, finding new ways to connect to their lands is crucial. "American Indians hold their lands—places—as having the highest possible meaning, and all their statements are made with this reference point in mind."[11] An Indigenous worldview is indivisible from the natural world; struggles to maintain and regenerate Indigenous languages and culture have been challenged by a separation from the physical places that give context and deeper layers of meaning to Indigenous language and culture.[12] VR and associated technologies may provide a way to bridge the separation between place and language by creating new kinds of place-based reference. A corollary question we will explore in the final year (summer 2022–23) of the grant concerns VR in K–12 language revitalization curriculum: how do we make VR an agent for active learning, as opposed to passive listening, for language learners just beginning their journeys toward language revitalization? The NALCC and language teachers in K–12 schools on Wind River, especially at the Arapaho Immersion School, will be instrumental in helping craft age- and language-level appropriate curricular materials for active VR language learning in the classroom.

In an effort to employ a decolonizing Indigenous methodology, the individual technologies that make up VR elicitation and the unspoken messages they carry must be critically interrogated. VR technology, 8,000-pixel 3D 360-degree panoramas, and aerial drone video used as tools to produce a VR application all leave their imprints. The impact of the technology and communications media we use and ingest on a daily basis is at once massive and often imperceptible. In the same way that we do not think about our legs, arms, hands, and voices per se as we go about our daily lives, we are also often not consciously aware of the tools we use, such as the internet, cellphones, augmented reality, and VR. Media philosopher Marshall McLuhan believed that communications media and technology were equivalent and in effect "extensions of man" and as such they extend the power of humans to become "living vortices of power" that often have unforeseen and negative effects on people as individuals, cultures, and society at large.[13] In the words of McLuhan, "The message of any medium or technology is the change of scale or pace or pattern that it introduces into human affairs" and so the message of our particular use of VR as a technological extension of humans is one of reclaiming ownership of Indigenous lands.[14]

VR has been used as tool in Indigenous language revitalization: for example, the Virtual Atoll Task, the WordsEye Linguistics Tool and the Digital Songlines Project have successfully explored the use of virtual simulations of people, places, and things.[15] The current project uses high-resolution 3D 360 images and video of actual locations and things rendered in VR to provide a highly realistic elicitation experience. Other examples of VR being used in Indigenous language teaching and learning include the VR spaces in Second Life created to teach dialects of Sámi. The use of VR in Sami language revitalization is focused on virtually connecting speakers of Sámi who are physically separated from each other to reestablish a sense of community, which has been shown to have a positive effect on the language-learning process.[16]

Technology itself is often far from benign or unintentionally exploitative, as the Indigenous Data Sovereignty and Data for Black Lives Matter movements have demonstrated. The very programs and algorithms that drive our digital culture are racially and culturally biased. Algorithms and data are never neutral; examples of bias in criminal risk assessment and predictive policing policies are only a few of the most recent examples of bias in consumer technology and the data that drives and informs it.[17] Pivotally, the effect of media and technology is often much greater than the content it carries and so, as McLuhan noted long ago, the medium is (or becomes) the message. McLuhan's assertions are even more relevant today than when they sprung into public and academic consciousness in 1965. However, a medium would be useless without a message and vice versa; Robert Logan's update of McLuhan's maxim is more apt in this current digital age: "The medium is the message and content is king!"[18] In sum, the use of any Western technology owned by institutions or individuals from a group that has historically dominated an Indigenous group has connotations in terms of the unequal access to capital to purchase technology and the underlying reasons for that inequality.

**Virtual Reality**

The history and majority of mainstream use of VR is dominated by the creation of virtual fantasy worlds where the user is transported to places that have or could not in fact exist—as seen in the gaming and entertainment industries. VR elicitation employs immersive VR using goggles with spatial audio and is distinct from "3D" VR as employed in Hollywood movies; immersive VR envelops people in a full 360-degree optical and auditory surround. Until recently, VR has been used only by researchers in computer technology and relatively small groups of technophiles with the money to buy or make expensive headsets. From 2015 to 2020 VR has become available in relatively inexpensive toys and headsets for computer games. More recently, due to improvements in mobile phone video processing and improved mobile data speeds, VR experiences are now available on any smartphone with the addition of gogglelike blinders into which the phone is placed. In our estimation, VR elicitation does not only take users to fantasy worlds: it can provide Indigenous consultants access to locations in their traditional lands from which their families and ancestors were removed by force and genocide and that they now may not have the means or physical ability to visit.

A pivotal aspect of the message of VR is how much it privileges sight, "subordination to the visual really points toward the coordination (and domination) by the visual of our other bodily faculties and senses. VR privileges sight, and other senses play a subordinate role to it."[19] The message of VR is also bound up in the specific means by which VR privileges sight. Once you put VR goggles on, you are completely blocked out of where you physically are and given an experience of being somewhere else that is so compelling and powerful your body responds as if you were actually in that place.[20]

The ways that human beings have over time told stories, painted pictures, staged ceremonies and plays, shown photographs and movies, and recently viewed 360 panoramic photos and entered VR simulations can be viewed as a continuum. The continuum reaches from experiences that took place in an intimate social setting where we were physically close to one another, listening to a person who was likely a family member a few feet away tell a story, to VR simulations that disconnect people completely from everyone and everything in their physical surroundings. This continuum places the intimate, social, unmediated experience on one end and the solitary, technology-mediated experience on the other. The message of VR could then easily be said to be one of isolation and technological dependency, and it surely is in many of its current applications. However, examples of VR are being used to connect people to one another and to places, for example VR productions by charities and nongovernmental organizations to tell and show the stories of the world's most vulnerable people. The United Nations Clouds Over Sidra simulation allows people to experience life in a Jordanian refugee camp.[21] Currently more uses of VR lean toward isolation than toward social connection, and yet the affordances of the medium itself make VR a powerful tool to promote empathy and connectedness. Importantly, VR elicitation improves on older VR technology that surrounded users with artificial models of an environment that were compelling only because they appeared to be real. VR elicitation is compelling because it uses high resolution 8K 3D panoramic photographs and video of real physical environments.[22] The VR elicitation prototype immerses people in 8K 3D 360 panoramic video and photography of real places with hyper-realistic three-dimensional detail down to the individual hairs on a buffalo robe. Simulations created from older VR technology are flat and artificial in comparison.

## 360 Panoramic Photography and Video

The history and practice of photography as a medium cannot be separated from the reality of its colonial gaze, appropriating power and othering the exotic.[23] In colonial Africa, the process of taking pictures of colonized people and lands and then distributing them back to colonial centers of power was a key part of the historic and ongoing processes of colonialism.[24] The camera was and arguably still is

> a triumph of Euro-American technology; controlled by whites; able to capture—and at the same time to rearrange the appearance of exotic environments and peoples; the camera played many roles. It created "landscapes"; it constructed the idea of "wildlife"; it produced stereotypical illustrations of "tribe" and "race."[25]

All photography and videography bear the imprint of the person taking the picture. The medium gives the photographer the ability to at once distance themselves from a person or place of interest, to construct an image that conforms to their ideals and ideology, and retain that image permanently—imparting a sense of power, control, and ownership over other people, places, and things. It is difficult to overstate how much the message contained in the medium of photography is or can be one of control, domination, and appropriation. As in colonial Africa, the history of photography in the western United States was inextricably part of the process of manifest destiny, territorial appropriation, othering, and genocide on both a physical and cultural level. Even more important to the specific context of our project is the fact that photography and videography are still in many ways the provenance of Euro-America; they are not available or utilized by members of the Northern Arapaho tribe nearly as much as they are by researchers or the media. In the very act of taking a photo or a video of a Native American today we can hear the echoes of salvage anthropology, appropriation, and exotic othering.

360 panoramic photography and videography carry many of the same messages and history of photography but are distinct in that a 360 panorama in VR becomes much more than a picture on a wall or a digital image or video on a flat two-dimensional screen. In VR, 360 panoramas become immersive experiences that give the viewer the sense that they are standing in that place, thereby subverting the traditional subject-object relationships between the viewer and the viewed present in traditional two-dimensional photography and video. When a 360 panorama or virtually any photo is taken on a smart device it is automatically combined with Global Positioning System (GPS) locational data derived by measuring the time it takes to receive radio signals from four or more satellites floating overhead. The worldwide web is now full of 360 panoramas with GPS data, most prominently on Google Earth, which allows anyone to see millions of physical locations on the globe without being there.

Mapping and spatial technologies like GPS can be seen as extensions of the colonial project of map making that has named and thereby asserted its power across the globe. GPS has the further connotation of being originally developed and still maintained in large part by the U.S. military. In a world where we can instantaneously reach out through the internet to see, explore, and appropriate a huge percentage of the earth, how can that technology in the context of Indigenous People and lands be seen as anything other than an extension of the exploring colonial gaze? It is truly frightening how quickly and easily web-based technologies "often reimagine colonialist practices by eliding Indigenous concerns about culturally appropriate conditions for access."[26]

### Drone Video

Drone videography carries the history and connotations of photography and cannot be separated from the history and messages of drones themselves. Drones, or unmanned aerial vehicles, were first employed by the Austrian military in its siege of Venice in 1849 when it sent balloons loaded with explosives to drop into the city. Later that century, military reconnaissance techniques in the Spanish-American War were developed that used early versions of cameras attached to kites. Since then, the technology has been continuously refined by the U.S. military and others to its present form of lethal surveillance; moreover, use of these surveillance technologies has become the general practice of security and control employed by nation-states around the world.[27] However, drone videography can become something else entirely in the hands of a documentary filmmaker or activist. For example, the stunning images of wild nature and endangered animals captured by drones give people a window into parts of our planet that they often cannot (and more importantly never should) visit—this is done to protect those places and the plant and animal life they support. More important here are the ways that drones have recently been used by Indigenous activists to document abuses of state power. The most prominent example of Indigenous drone activism is the extensive use of drones by the activists at Standing Rock, North Dakota, in their opposition to the proposed Dakota Access Pipeline (DAPL). DAPL construction threatened Lakota cultural and sacred sites and Standing Rock's sovereignty because the pipeline would bring more than five hundred thousand barrels of oil under Lake Oahe, the only source of drinking water for the Standing Rock Sioux Nation and millions of others downstream. The activists were pitted against militarized police, National Guard roadblocks, heavy surveillance from local, state, and federal forces; they used drone technology to document the militarized force and brutality being perpetrated upon them and then broadcast images of that brutality around the world.[28] Drone video footage is also becoming a tool for global Indigenous Peoples to protect their lands and strengthen their claims to that land.[29] Drone technology may have a militaristic message in society in general, but it is being increasingly utilized in ways that run counter to that message.

Academic research on Indigenous Peoples has traditionally been a largely extractive process whereby unique worldviews, knowledge, and languages have been collected, removed, and then studied in academic contexts. Each layer of this extractive process has been in large part facilitated by Euro-Western technologies from the pen to the aerial drone. We strive to find new and restorative processes that use these same technologies to return places and knowledge to Indigenous communities while challenging tired stereotypes that find use of cutting-edge technology by Indigenous Peoples "unexpected," implausible, or somehow unnatural.[30]

## Part III: COVID-19, Research, and Data Sovereignty

With the emergence of COVID-19 our elder Northern Arapaho collaborators and all members of the NALCC went into isolation to protect themselves from contracting the virus and the project ground to a halt. We were forced to search yet again for new ways to reconnect places and knowledge to Indigenous communities. The process had unforeseen consequences that engendered a deeper decolonization of our research methodology: during the spring of 2020 in collaboration with the campus 3D visualization center we developed a mobile version of our Buffalo Roads VR elicitation application that could be run on a mobile phone with a portable VR headset. Mobile VR kits could be sent directly to our collaborators without any risk of transmission of COVID-19, removing us physically from the process. Our original work plan had required the physical presence of at least two of our project team to run both the VR application via a desktop or laptop computer and record the elders as they talked about the places they were visiting in VR. Over the summer and early fall of 2020 two Northern Arapaho elders were able to virtually visit the Buffalo Roads and record their knowledge and language in a way that was safe and convenient to them. This new method placed the locus of control over every aspect of the language elicitation sessions firmly in the hands of the elders themselves: the elders were able to explore the locations in private and at will. The sessions were successful in moving the project forward. One elder speaker remarked "I feel happy because I see these things, what all I am seeing right now I feel happy due to this. A long time ago, these places, that was where all the Arapahos lived, . . . They looked for buffalo. . . . It's like I just feel I am present here again, like an Arapaho. I am an Arapaho."

At the time of writing, we are working on recording the five locales and collecting relevant hunting stories. A growing concern in Indigenous studies is data ownership, storage, and the problems that arise with data collection in Indigenous communities: Who owns the data? Who stores the data? How is that data used and who has access to it? Here are some of our data sovereignty procedures:

- In accordance with the NALCC wishes, upon completion of the project all data will be archived with the Sam Noble Native American Languages Collection and at the University of Wyoming American Heritage Center in perpetuity. Both archives have an ongoing and trusted relationship with the tribe.
- In accordance with NALCC wishes, all materials in both archives will be freely available. The Sam Noble Native American Languages Collection will also make the materials freely available on their website.
- We will donate all equipment, VR software applications, and all curricular materials funded by the grant to the NALCC and whatever schools on the Wind River Reservation request these materials.
- The only foreseeable exception to the above stipulations is data containing drone video of places or people where permission was not secured ahead of time or given after request. Such material will be deleted.

Ultimately, this project represents a small but necessary step *toward* fully immersive VR language applications—VR video games—where the user/player must be able to understand, use, and speak an Indigenous language to progress through the game. We hope to see in our lifetimes VR games where we have to speak tribal languages and understand tribal cultures and protocols in order to progress through the game. Can a VR video game become an *authentic* cultural experience? It may be time to redefine the authentic.

As we prepared to leave Buffalo Roads and the Fortress that day in September 2019, we could not help but think of the difference between the two names (Fortress and Buffalo Roads) both of which were recently placed upon the landscape. The name *Fortress*, which nonnative anthropologists applied to the stone monolith, implies a military stronghold and a martial, aggressive worldview. It also denotes a barricading from the outside world. As such, perhaps it says more about the anthropologists' view of precolonized Indigenous People than it does about any Indigenous reality past or present. The Buffalo Roads, which was the name the Arapaho gave to the area near the Fortress, implies movement, connection among living worlds, and ties between the Indigenous People and the buffalo. We cannot help but wonder what name the Arapaho elders would have given the Fortress if the anthropologists had not already signified it, if the Arapaho were allowed to spend time on the now private ranch and get to know the area once again. We walked one last time through the Buffalo Roads themselves, the trenches cut into the lithified clay and bedrock by the millions of buffalo hooves migrating through the area over the thousands of years. We, too, carried away a little clay on our feet.

PHINEAS KELLY is a postdoctoral researcher at the University of Wyoming. He bears close ties of kinship to Rapa Nui, whose Polynesian people, culture, and language all constitute an essential dimension of his identity. Kelly currently collaborates with both the Northern Arapaho Tribe and the Rapa Nui to revitalize and regenerate Indigenous language and culture.

CHRIS CASKEY RUSSELL is originally from Seattle and is an enrolled member of the Tlingit tribe of Alaska. He is the dean of Fairhaven College of Interdisciplinary Studies at Western Washington University.

## References

Arora, Gabo, and Chris Milk. *Clouds over Sidra*. 2015; Za'atari Refugee Camp, Jordan. Accessed February 12, 2021. https://docubase.mit.edu/project/clouds-over-sidra/.

Basso, Keith H. *Wisdom Sits in Places: Landscape and Language Among the Western Apache*. Albuquerque: University of New Mexico Press, 1996.

Caldecott, Marion, and Karsten Koch. "Using Mixed Media Tools for Eliciting Discourse in Indigenous Languages." *Language Documentation & Conservation* 8 (2014): 209–40.

Christen, Kimberly. "Does Information Really Want to be Free? Indigenous Knowledge Systems and the Question of Openness." *International Journal of Communication* 6 (2012): 2870–93.

Cowell, Andrew, and Alonzo Moss Sr. *The Arapaho language*. Boulder: University Press of Colorado, 2011.

Deloria, Philip Joseph. *Indians in Unexpected Places*. Lawrence: University Press of Kansas, 2004.

Deloria, Vine. *God is Red: A Native View of Religion*. Colorado: Fulcrum, 2003.

Hartmann, Wolfram, Jeremy Silvester, and Patricia Hayes, eds. *The Colonising Camera: Photographs in the Making of Namibian History*. Cape Town: Juta and Company, 1999.

Hillis, Ken. *Digital Sensations: Space, Identity, and Embodiment in Virtual Reality*. Minneapolis: University of Minnesota Press, 1999.

Kindervater, Katharine Hall. "The Emergence of Lethal Surveillance: Watching and Killing in the History of Drone Technology." *Security Dialogue* 47, no. 3 (2016): 223–38.

Leavy, Brett. "Digital Songlines: Digitizing the Arts, Culture and Heritage Landscape of Aboriginal Australia." In *Information Technology and Indigenous People,* edited by Laurel Evelyn Dyson, Max Hendricks, and Stephen Grant, 159–69. Pennsylvania: IGI Global, 2007.

Logan, Robert K. *Understanding New Media: Extending Marshall McLuhan.* New York: Peter Lang, 2010.

Lum, Jonathon, and Jonathan Schlossberg. "The Virtual Atoll Task: A Spatial Language Elicitation Tool." In *The 45th Australian Linguistic Society Conference Proceedings,* edited by Mark Harvey, 82–103. Newcastle, Australia: University of Newcastle Press, 2014.

McLuhan, Marshall. *Understanding Media: The Extensions of Man.* Cambridge, MA: MIT Press, 1994.

O'Neil, Cathy. *Weapons of Math Destruction: How Big Data Increases Inequality and Threatens Democracy.* New York: Crown, 2016.

Outakoski, Hanna. "Teaching an Endangered Language in Virtual Reality." In *Keeping Languages Alive: Documentation, Pedagogy and Revitalization,* edited by Mari C. Jones and Sarah Ogilvie, 128–139. Cambridge: Cambridge University Press, 2013.

Paneque-Gálvez, Jaime, Nicolás Vargas-Ramírez, Brian M. Napoletano, and Anthony Cummings. "Grassroots Innovation Using Drones for Indigenous Mapping and Monitoring." *Land* 6, no. 4 (2017): 86.

Ranger, Terence. "Colonialism, Consciousness and the Camera." *Past & Present* 171 (2001): 203–215.

Rony, Fatimah Tobing. *The Third Eye: Race, Cinema, and Ethnographic Spectacle.* Durham, NC: Duke University Press, 1996.

Smith, Linda Tuhiwai. *Decolonizing methodologies: Research and Indigenous Peoples, 2nd Edition.* London: Zed Books, 2013.

Tuck, Sarah. "Drone Vision and Protest." *Photographies* 11, no. 2–3 (2018): 169–75.

Ulinski, Morgan, Anusha Balakrishnan, Daniel Bauer, Bob Coyne, Julia Hirschberg, and Owen Rambow. "Documenting Endangered Languages with the Wordseye Linguistics Tool." In *Proceedings of the 2014 Workshop on the Use of Computational Methods in the Study of Endangered Languages,* edited by Jeff Good, Julia Hirschberg, and Owen Rambow, 6–14. Baltimore: Association for Computational Linguistics, 2014.

Yu, Chia-Pin, Hsiao-Yun Lee, and Xiang-Yi Luo. "The Effect of Virtual Reality Forest and Urban Environments on Physiological and Psychological Responses." *Urban Forestry & Urban Greening* 35 (2018): 106–14.

## Notes

1. The members of the NALCC who collaborated most often on the project are Wayne C'Hair, Nii'eihii Neecee, Ray Underwood, and Marian Scott.

2. The family who owns the land has asked we not provide location names, coordinates, or anything specific that can identify the area and potentially bring souvenir hunters onto their land.

3. The Sand Creek Massacre took place on November 29, 1864, in what is now southeast Colorado. The Third Colorado Cavalry under the command of John Chivington massacred hundreds of Cheyenne and Arapaho men, women, and children, mutilating and desecrating their bodies afterward.

4. The Buffalo Roads area is located on a private ranch owned by a nonnative family. The ranch is fenced and the access to the Buffalo Roads is difficult—it must be done on foot or with an ATV. As such, the Buffalo Roads, for all intents and purposes, remains off-limits to visitors.

5. Cowell and Moss Sr., *The Arapaho language,* 2—7.

6. The authors already had a good working relationship with the NALCC. Wayne C'Hair of the NALCC had been instrumental in setting up our university's Northern Arapaho language courses. We reached out to him for permission to demonstrate our VR project at the weekly NALCC meeting.

7. A major component of our research depends on elicitation sessions with the NALCC and others—especially language learners. With the help of the NALCC members, we have created a series of questions in Northern Arapaho to ask participants while they are wearing the VR gear.

8. Elders use the term "their language" when speaking about Northern Arapaho even when referring to younger generations, whose first language is English. There is still a very real sense that English is not *their* language. Rather, English is an interloper and eventually the Northern Arapaho will return to speaking and using Northern Arapaho as their main language.

9. Smith, *Decolonizing Methodologies,* 63.

10. Smith, *Decolonizing Methodologies,* 41.

11. Deloria, *God is Red,* 61.

12. Basso, *Wisdom Sits in Places,* 110.

13. McLuhan, *Understanding Media,* 22.

14. McLuhan, *Understanding Media,* 8.

15. Lum and Schlossberg, "The Virtual Atoll," 82—103; Ulinski et al., "Words-eye Linguistics Tool," 6—14; Brett Leavy, "Digital Songlines" 159—69.

16. Outakoski, "Teaching an Endangered," 128—39.

17. O'Neil, *Weapons of Math Destruction,* 84—105.

18. Logan, *Understanding New Media,* 354.

19. Hillis, *Digital Sensations,* 35.

20. Yu, Lee, and Luo, "Effect of Virtual," 106—14.

21. Arora and Milk, *Clouds over Sidra.*

22. The term "8K" refers to the high-resolution camera's ability to digitally capture video at an approximate width of eight thousand pixels.

23. Tobing Rony, "*The Third Eye,*" 77—99.

24. Hartmann, Silvester, and Hayes, eds., *The Colonising Camera.*

25. Ranger, "Colonialism, Consciousness," 203—15.

26. Christen, "Does Information Really," 2870—93.

27. Kindervater, "Emergence of Lethal," 223—38.

28. Tuck, "Drone Vision," 169—75.

29. Paneque-Gálvez et al., "Grassroots Innovation," 86.

30. Deloria, *Indians in Unexpected,* 183—224.

# SHERYL LIGHTFOOT

*Rhetoric and Settler Inertia: Strategies of Canadian Decolonization*
by Patrick Belanger
Rowman & Littlefield, 2019

*Arts of Engagement: Taking Aesthetic Action in and Beyond Canada's
    Truth and Reconciliation Commission*
by Dylan Robinson and Keavy Martin
Wilfrid Laurier University Press, 2016

*Research & Reconciliation: Unsettling Ways of Knowing through
    Indigenous Relationships*
by Shawn Wilson, Andrea V. Breen, and Lindsay Dupré
Canadian Scholars, 2019

**SINCE 2015**, when the Truth and Reconciliation Commission of Canada (TRC) issued its Final Report and 94 Calls to Action, which described the proper pathway for reconciliation in Canada, there has been a virtual explosion of academic literature on how the TRC's Calls to Action can and should be operationalized. Many have taken the position that reconciliation—and decolonization—must be Indigenous directed, while also holding settler society primarily responsible and accountable for most of the actions that reconciliation requires. Numerous scholars also hold that academia, especially its research function, have a key role to play in reconciliation processes. This collection of three books advances both ideas.

Patrick Belanger opens his book *Rhetoric and Settler Inertia* by asking how rhetoric can aid in the decolonial process, primarily as a tool to persuade settlers who are resistant to change. Amid a wider body of literature about decolonial rhetoric and settler response, Belanger explores forms of rhetoric *and* methods of delivery that impact settlers' willingness to change in pursuit of decolonization. Belanger concludes that rhetoric focused on interest convergence (mutual benefit) lends possible advantages to the decolonial project that dialogue and education neglect. Working within an "X leads to Y" framework in which X is decolonial rhetoric and Y is settler action, Belanger identifies Z (mutual benefit) as a spurious variable. Accordingly, Belanger aims to reveal that settler buy-in to decolonization could accelerate the process of decolonization—as outlined by Indigenous nations—in demands for restitution. Belanger affirms that decolonization must be led by Indigenous People and seeks to determine whether "public reason might, through communication, triumph over money and violence" (96). Belanger's proposed path for achieving this end is for rhetorical frameworks to facilitate interest convergence.

*Rhetoric and Settler Inertia* usefully examines theoretical rhetorical work in practice and expands the boundaries of what rhetoric captures. It is interesting to consider whether rhetoric can be a tool for acknowledging responsibility and constructing a decolonial, or less colonial, future. Belanger's emphasis on an Indigenous-centered approach to reconciliation is worth noting but, regardless, this book is focused on how reconciliation can best appeal to settlers.

In *Arts of Engagement,* Dylan Robinson and Keavy Martin examine the TRC through a critical lens focused on aesthetic action: "how a range of sensory stimuli—image, sound, and movement—have social and political effects through our affective engagements with them" (2). This book examines the relationship between the TRC, aesthetic action, and political change. Together, contributors to *Arts of Engagement* tell the stories of the TRC and art, demonstrating that aesthetics can serve to distance or reconcile two groups; art can be either superficial or a recognition of epistemologically and ontologically relevant Indigenous-led healing.

*Arts of Engagement* draws on qualitative evidence and is focused on art completed or witnessed by the authors. The evidence and case studies chosen were tangible and prominent, letting readers draw on their own conceptions of art. Many Indigenist methodologies were employed, even by the predominantly settler authors. The book's larger argument is that large-scale institutional and societal transformation happens not only in the mind but in the body. Thus, recognizing Indigenous process to reconciliation is necessary for actual reconciliation to occur. The editors and authors aim to show the ways in which aesthetic actions are essential to Indigenous ontologies and therefore to truth-telling, law-making, and reconciliation.

In the anthology *Research & Reconciliation: Unsettling Ways of Knowing through Indigenous Relationships*, editors Shawn Wilson, Andrea V. Brazen, and Lindsay Dupré explore reconciliatory experiences in relation to diverse research methods. They argue that Indigenist research methods are "based on an understanding that reality is relationships" (8–9) and that knowledge produced by relationships is credible and relevant for researchers in the social sciences and beyond. Their primary objective is to challenge Eurocentric conceptions of research, and its facilitators, with the aim that researchers will use their power and knowledge to challenge the status quo. The book includes three sections—"Being, Longing, and Belonging," "No Fucking Thanks-Giving," and "Learning to Walk"—and is divided into seventeen chapters, interspliced with articles from satire-news source *Walking Eagle News*.

Every author in *Research & Reconciliation* focuses on Indigenist research, emphasizing and demonstrating a reciprocal relationship with their subjects. The evidence presented is entirely qualitative and often anecdotal. Each chapter engages with different methodologies: transcription, storytelling, interview, personal essay, creative writing, poetry, and so on, often blending one into another. Focusing on both domestic and international stories, the book has a wide geographic scope and showcases a range of diverse views and experiences. Overall, the collection embodies its thesis: Indigenist research that engages with relational accountability is itself an act of reconciliation, as is this anthology. Among its strengths, *Research & Reconciliation* can claim diverse research methods that are demonstrated for readers. Of the many contributors, each provides nuance that helps to broaden the reader's understanding of the parameters of Indigenist research and Indigenist methodologies, illustrating a commendable balance of perspectives.

In sum, while *Research & Reconciliation* notes that not all Indigenous researchers use Indigenist methodologies, nor do Indigenist methodologies exclude non-Indigenous researchers, it clarifies that Indigenist ontology centers the understanding that reality *is* relationships. Rather than individuals acting within relationships, this book asserts that relationships define individual players. Thus, for research, a relational understanding requires acknowledgment of researchers' relationships to their work and the world around them. Largely, Indigenist research methods are essential in the academic space for reconciliation to occur, and research is—or can be—reconciliation.

All three of these books would be appropriate for graduate and advanced undergraduate courses in critical Indigenous studies, cultural studies, Indigenous research methods, and Indigenous political theory courses.

SHERYL LIGHTFOOT (Anishinaabe) is associate professor in the Department of Political Science and the School of Public Policy and Global Affairs, associate faculty in the Institute for Critical Indigenous Studies, senior advisor to the president on Indigenous affairs, and Canada Research Chair in Global Indigenous Rights and Politics at the University of British Columbia.

# BEVERLEY DIAMOND

*Hungry Listening: Resonant Theory for Indigenous Sound Studies*
by Dylan Robinson
University of Minnesota Press, 2020

HUNGRY LISTENING examines intercultural performances by or with Indigenous musicians. Robinson discusses how classical concerts, where music is presented for aesthetic contemplation, contrast with Indigenous practices that speak back to colonial institutions and values. The format and content of the book are equally innovative. Both chapters and creative interventions (poetry, event scores) between chapters speak to the themes of intersubjectivity, performative writing, encounters between Indigenous and early music, ethnographic redress, and reconciliation. Questioning entitlement and reconfiguring "structures of inclusion" (6), Robinson asks settler readers not to read a short chapter entitled "Writing Indigenous Space."

Robinson describes two examples that demonstrate the central themes. Euro-American assumptions that music is aesthetic enrichment contrast with Indigenous uses of song as law, medicine, or primary historical documentation. To illustrate, the author examines the transcript of the British Columbia land claims case *Delgamuukw v. the Queen,* when Judge McEachern, claiming a "tin ear," refused to allow song in his courtroom, denying song as oral history and legal order that brings memory back into a territory. Another settler refusal emerged in the moving story of a visit to Saint Olave's Church (London, UK) where Peter Morin asked to sing to the spirit of an Indigenous child captured by Frobisher and buried in St. Olave's. Told he could not sing or speak, Morin undertook a silent ceremony mimicking drum beating to honor the child.

The following "Event Score for Guest Listening" contemplates Kingston, Ontario, a city known for limestone buildings that symbolize the weight of settler permanence. "Writing about Musical Intersubjectivity," turns to intellectuals who "seek forms of writing otherwise" (103). Indigenous models—for example, Leanne Simpson's multigenre publications (academic writing, storytelling, or music recording); Lee Maracle's "Conversations . . ."; and narratives of Residential School survivors—are curiously not referenced. A section on "spatial intersubjectivity" contrasts the land as sentient with museum spaces (96). Robinson makes no mention of more enlightened museum practices, as stewards not owners, and enablers of Indigenous care and use of artifacts on museum or community premises. Related, though in stark contrast, is the interlude on Raven Chacon's *Report,* a composition for gunshot ensemble.

Chapter 3 considers concert works that imagine sound worlds of first contact between Indigenous custodians of the land and settler arrivals. Inuit throat singing—concert music's frequent "go to" genre for Indigenous sound—may resonate with classical musicians' interest in experimental vocal techniques but more likely because it is marked as "exotic." Composers' approaches vary from integration, to trading, to sonic displays of starkly juxtaposed styles that emphasize sharp differences. An "Event Score for Those Who Hold Our Songs" follows, urging collectors to give the songs back. Although some museum/community collaborations have helped bring songs to life again—for example, the Haida Nation publication of boxed sets of *Songs of Haida Gwai,* Mi'kmaq CDs of the recordings of Mechling—there is much more to be done.

Appropriation by settler composers is addressed further in "Ethnographic Redress, Compositional Responsibility." Alongside are Indigenous initiatives: Mike Dangeli's "Temporary Longhouse for Ethnographic Redress," where the gifting of song gives hope and serves as witness to truth; Peter Morin's singing "to sites of colonial power"; and Cheryl l'Hirondelle's "Why the Caged Bird Sings" informed by visits with incarcerated Indigenous women.

Alexina Louie's "Take the Dog Sled," for throat singers and chamber ensemble, on the other hand, is described as "sound tourism" that ignores the killing of sled dogs to discourage travel on the land, a history unfolded during the Qikiqtani Truth Commission. That troubled history emerges in the postchapter interlude where Robinson suggests a recasting of Louie's work with projected images of statements about the enforced killing of dogs filmed by Indigenous youth. Robinson also suggests a restaging: having the audience walk through an open space (not on stage) where throat singers are performing.

The final chapter, "Feeling Reconciliation," makes clear that recognition is not enough. The orientation of multiculturalism toward "friendly coming together" and "easily digestible narratives" is problematized as an avoidance of "listening in relation," which is often agonistic in its address of social inequity (204). Adding to the literature on problematic representations of Indigeneity at the Olympics, the chapter focuses on the 2010 Vancouver games where Indigenous performers were part of the branding of national identity. He critiques multicultural display as a poor substitute for nation-to-nation relations.

Robinson reflects on the airing of Bill Reid's film *Beyond Eden* about the removal of Haida poles in 1957 to place them in the Museum of Anthropology, poles that Haida had decided to return to the earth. The story moved many to weep, but Robinson observes that "affect and efficacy" should not be conflated (217).

Finally, Robinson considers the Getting' Higher Choir's joyful performance of Susan Aglukark's "O Siem" at a Truth and Reconciliation (TRC) regional event. The clash between the history of residential school abuse and the choir's celebratory stance that "we are all the same" was disturbing (225).

The concluding chapter returns to the topic of dialogue and relationship building, stressing again that both together-and-apart formats, as well as exclusive conversations, are essential. He takes the bold step of asking two settler colleagues with whom he discussed the manuscript to write in response to his ideas.

I hope readers will further the discussion of concepts Robinson introduces: (1) The contrasting contexts of "hunger": Do stereotypes resemble starvation? When is listening healthy? Is listening always carnivorous?; (2) "Refusal": as ignorance, exacerbating anger, or opening hearts and minds to what is irreconcilable or inaccessible? Such questions might encourage new approaches to listening against the grain.

**BEVERLEY DIAMOND** is an ethnomusicologist and Professor Emerita at Memorial University of Newfoundland.

# CAROLINE WIGGINTON

*Time of Anarchy: Indigenous Power and the Crisis of Colonialism
    in Early America*
by Matthew Kruer
Harvard University Press, 2021

WHO WERE THE SUSQUEHANNOCKS? Most scholars of seventeenth-century eastern
North America have encountered the name of this Indigenous confederacy—
whose territories during this period were primarily in what is now Virginia—
in colonial records, but no contemporary tribal nation self-identifies using
this name or any of its other endo- and exonymns, such as Minqua, Gandas-
togue, or Andastes. Today, Susquehannock descendants live among Lenape,
Haudenosaunee, and other peoples rather than constituting an autonomous
tribal nation. Yet, as Matthew Kruer's deeply archival historiography *Time of
Anarchy* shows, Susquehannock was a small nation which, through its network of relationships, held influence "out of proportion to its numbers" (4).
As he explains, from 1675 to 1685 (the titular "time of anarchy"), Susquehannocks "connect[ed]" to "dozens of peoples and colonies in a spasm of
conflict that washed over eastern North America" (4). Kruer asserts that his
"book tells, for the first time, the history of the Susquehannock migrations
and their ramifications in the English colonies" (6).

Time of Anarchy begins with Virginia and the region's seventeenth-
century Native and colonial context, including an overview of the limited
knowledge scholars have regarding the Susquehannock. Subsequently, the
book becomes what is often a martial and political history of the late 1600s,
one that explains the role that mid-Atlantic Indigenous peoples, especially
but not only the Susquehannocks, played in conflicts as well as social and
political realignments. Of the events Kruer narrates through a Susquehannock lens, Bacon's Rebellion (1676—77), which pitted factions of Virginia's
Black and white newcomers against each other and against Native peoples,
is arguably the most studied; one of its early signal incidents was an assault
by Nathaniel Bacon's Volunteers on Occaneechi Island and its Native inhabitants, a battle that led to what Kruer evocatively terms the "Susquehannock
Scattering." Chapter 3 and beyond follow the trails and effects of the scattering south, north, and west as well as within Virginia. Through the Susquehannock Scattering, Kruer connects far-flung events from Carolina to New
York, Quebec, and the Haudenosaunee Confederacy. These events parallel

those of Metacom's War (1675–78) in northeastern North America, as brilliantly narrated by Lisa Brooks (Abenaki) in *Our Beloved Kin: Remapping A New History of King Philip's War* (2019).

Though the title refers to settler colonial descriptions of this decade (6), the thread that may interest *NAIS* readers who research this period and region is Susquehannock maintenance of order in the midst of cataclysmic disorder. Though fragmented, the Susquehannocks continued by relying on a network of relationships. Even as they scattered, they merged, transformed, and confederated. *NAIS* readers may also be interested in the many other interconnected Native peoples and figures, one of which, in another parallel to *Our Beloved Kin,* is an influential and savvy woman leader, in this instance Pamunkey weroansqua Cockacoeske (156–63).

So far, this review might suggest that *Time of Anarchy* is a book about the Susquehannocks. And it is. But it is simultaneously a book about Bacon's Rebellion, late seventeenth-century Virginia and mid-Atlantic colonial politics, and the region's Indigenous peoples. Methodologically, it is an historiography, organized chronologically, which relies on an astounding array of documentary sources compiled from dozens of U.S. and British collections. But with each chapter, it also "employs a different mode of analysis"—for example, emotional cultures, conspiracy theory, racial thinking—in order to activate diverse bodies of "interdisciplinary literature" and delineate how different "phenomena . . . drove different phases of the Time of Anarchy" (7). In addition to these modes—mostly drawn from outside NAIS—the book "interpret[s]" primary sources "through the lens of ethnohistory and the methods developed by scholars of Native American and Indigenous Studies" (9). For Kruer, this dual ethnohistorical-NAIS methodology means "using sources produced by Natives whenever possible and reading them with an eye toward Indigenous epistemologies." "It also requires," he continues, "using colonial documents without privileging colonial perspectives" (9). Kruer's implicit and explicit goals for this book, therefore, were admirably ambitious. However, the result may feel at times dense and uneven, with one thread, method, or mode of analysis being lost or overwhelmed as he pursues another and with NAIS methods and scholarship truncated, skimmed, and endnoted rather than foregrounded. The most memorable parts occur when Kruer tells the fascinating and necessary narrative of the Susquehannock people at the end of the seventeenth century. His work and its underlying archive in this regard will be of great importance and interest.

CAROLINE WIGGINTON is associate professor of English at the University of Mississippi.

# GLORIA E. CHACÓN

*Mayalogue: An Interactionist Theory of Indigenous Cultures*
by Victor Montejo
SUNY Press, 2021

VICTOR MONTEJO'S LATEST PUBLICATION, *Mayalogue: An Interactionist Theory of Indigenous Cultures*, represents a singular interweaving of Indigenous epistemology, science, prophecy, oral traditions, ontologies, calendars, and personal narrative. The book is a timely invitation to readers across fields to suspend their preconceived beliefs concerning truth, objectivity, and scientific methods. The discussion questions traditional disciplines about epistemology and Indigenous relationality. Montejo proposes a theory of "mayalogue" based on his own community that centers Indigenous Peoples' understanding of humans and nonhumans as part of the cosmic web of life or q'inal, which is translated as life, time, and existence. Montejo convincingly argues humanity needs to move away from scientific materialism to understanding Indigenous ways of relating to the nonhuman in order to save our world.

Mayalogue demands that the sciences seriously consider Indigenous Peoples' multidimensional approach encompassing economy, architecture, religion, agriculture, and the environment. Joined by the same breath, life represents a unifying power that maintains balance with all that exists on earth and the universe. His discussion offers us insights into Maya spirituality and knowledge of the cosmos and their condensation in stories. He convincingly demonstrates that creation stories are not just fiction but a daily practice that seeks to preserve the equilibrium between nature and humans in the universe. Montejo argues that in the process of worldling, Indigenous Peoples are aware of their collective role for moving toward a healthy direction and safeguarding the planet for future generations.

Montejo's intervention embodies a clarion call to shift our contemporary consciousness and turn to the teachings of Indigenous Peoples whose cautionary words and advice become increasingly relevant in the face of plagues, natural disasters, and wars. Achieving change requires rejecting our materialist value system and our current capitalist mode of relating to others. Mayalogue can best be described as trialogue where Indigenous Peoples embrace the totality in a continuous process of reciprocity. The triad explains Indigenous Peoples' cultivated interaction between humans, nature, and the supernatural world. His overarching methodology represents a native theory for synthesizing Maya knowledge and epistemology; it is about acknowledging and following the norms of intimate relationships with the land and the universe, a reciprocal action generated among humans, nature, and the supernatural world or ancestors who are considered guardian spirits. Montejo puts forth the concept of KOMONTAT, which is a jakaltek Maya term referring to a model of coordinating effort that unifies human activity with harvest production. Komontat responds to the needs of the community while honoring the ancestors during the gathering for religious festivities. In other words, kinship or relationality with everything that exists must be the guiding principle in our everyday life activities. Montejo emphasizes that for Native Americans, the concept of community is cosmo-centric and extends to all living beings on earth and beyond.

Among the many analytics Montejo shares, I found his "telescoping of time" particularly nuanced: a Native way of documenting historical events that are considered extraordinary and must be anchored in the mind of future generations for centuries or millennia (84). Telescoping supports re-analyzing *Popol Wuj* or *Chilám Balám.* Translated as *Book of Council* and the *Spokesperson of the Jaguar,* respectively, these postcontact documents chronicle the histories of the Mayan civilization, its cosmologies, traditions, and spirituality. Montejo observes that Maya cosmogenesis resulting from the struggle of the twins and their defeat of the lords of the underworld epitomizes Maya worldling as narrated in *Popol Wuj.* Chapter 9 offers rich and stimulating discussions on the spirit bearer of time, the quadrilateral universe, and cosmological differences between the Tonal (alter ego) and the Nawal (a person that uses their animal essence to practice harm)—two concepts that acquired different meanings over time. In contemporary Maya spiritual practices, tonal is no longer in use; instead, nawal (spirit or energy) or animal counterpart is more common. Despite this shift over time, for Montejo, the concept that a person with an animal counterpart forms a unit or a totality in life sharing the same destiny offers an important insight into a theory of the self as a framework by which a human or person possesses a dual human and animal essence and vice versa.

This book truly reflects an offering, a ceremony, to a new way of thinking about sharing and expanding our understanding of Mayan cosmology from the experience of a Maya scholar and writer who has lived and struggled between two worlds. Trained in anthropology, Montejo has the vantage point of having learned methods and theories from a field that has been controversial for Indigenous communities and to offer us his perspective as a Maya with other ways of knowing. This book returns to the mission passed down by the ancestors to Indigenous Peoples to nourish, remember, and understand our role in a complex web of relations.

GLORIA E. CHACÓN (Maya Ch'orti' and campesino origin) is associate professor in the Literature Department at University of California, San Diego.

# JESSICA L. SÁNCHEZ FLORES

*Indigenous Women and Violence: Feminist Activist Research in Heightened States of Injustice*
edited by Lynn Stephen and Shannon Speed
University of Arizona Press, 2021

**INDIGENOUS WOMEN AND VIOLENCE:** *Feminist Activist Research in Heightened States of Injustice* presents various experiences of Indigenous women from Mexico and Guatemala who have survived violence in settler capitalist states. Together, the contributing authors—predominantly Indigenous and Latinx/Mestiza—frame their work as "engaged, feminist, collaborative, and activist" (18). In their cowritten introduction, Speed (Chickasaw) and Stephen establish the institutionalization of racialized gender violence in settler states since colonization but counter this narrative with an exposition of the myriad ways Indigenous women have navigated legal contexts and other oppressive spaces as they seek justice.

In her chapter, Speed weaves together her own experience as a survivor of gender violence with the stories of Indigenous women in the detention center at Hutto, Texas. For her part, Stephen highlights the experiences of female Mam refugees from Guatemala seeking asylum in the United States and the discrimination and violence(s) encountered during their journey. In her contribution, R. Aída Hernández Castillo focuses on how incarcerated Indigenous and Mestiza women in central Mexico have created communities and found ways to write and publish their own stories. María Teresa Sierra studies how Indigenous women leaders known as *promotoras de justicia* (justice seekers) from the mountain region of Guerrero, Mexico, are generating bonds of trust to help women share their stories. At the same time, they are educating the male authorities in their communities so that they may be more open to recognizing and listening to women's demands. In her chapter, Irma A. Velásquez Nimatuj (Maya K'iche') documents and witnesses the stories of Q'eqchi' women who survived the brutal sexual violence by the state and the military in Sepur Zarco during the armed conflict. Maria Mora demonstrates intergenerational leadership and collective learning among Zapatista women in Chiapas, Mexico.

The two final chapters focus on Indigenous women and genocide. Morna Macleod provides an overview of her work with the Guatemalan Human

Rights Commission and the various tribunals that have allowed many women to denounce the genocide they experienced in the form of gendered and sexual violence. Unlike the other chapters, in the final chapter Margo Tamez (Ndé) uses creative writing to denounce the ongoing genocide of Ndé (Lipan Apache) people of El Calaboz on the U.S./Mexico border. In the epilogue Speed and Stephen discuss the impact of the COVID-19 pandemic on Indigenous women, particularly related to their increased exposure to violence during the pandemic.

A common thread throughout the volume is the analysis of gender violence from an intersectional standpoint that considers race, class, gender, and sexuality and how this violence is repeatedly allowed by settler capitalist structures. The authors frame emotional knowledges as a tool to help scholars who work with Indigenous women acknowledge their emotions as well as those felt by the women who have been exposed to multiple violence(s). As scholars we need to center our emotions because it impacts how we process and share those stories. Centering their own emotions throughout the volume, the authors also acknowledge the pain, frustration, rage, hatred, and trauma they have felt related to the stories shared with them.

In each chapter the authors thoughtfully share their own ways of self-care and the interlocutors' processes for healing. As Hernández Castillo asserts, "We need to work with this pain . . . from a caring language that allows us to heal and continue constructing community" (67). Through their experiences we learn that there is no single recipe to follow, sometimes self-care and healing will manifest by speaking to an audience, with meditation, in a *temazcal* (Mesoamerican steam bath), with rituals, or with writing. We need to take care of our body, mind, soul, and spirit in order to be present for everyone who is a survivor of gender violence and those who work with gender violence and Indigenous women.

This volume is appropriate for college courses in various disciplines such as Native American/Indigenous studies, women and gender studies, Latin American studies, and sociocultural anthropology. It invites further scholarly discussion about the ways in which scholars attend to their emotions in their ethnographic work and writing, self-care when there is secondary trauma or retraumatization, and the ways scholars can collaborate with Indigenous women to heal from those traumatic experiences. With this in mind, this volume serves as a model for the ways in which we can challenge and imagine new ways to conduct Indigenous feminist embodied activist research across borders.

JESSICA L. SÁNCHEZ FLORES (Nahua descent) is a Ph.D. candidate in the Department of Spanish and Portuguese at the University of Texas at Austin.

# THERESA STEWART-AMBO

*A Coalition of Lineages: The Fernandeño Tataviam Band of Mission Indians*
by Duane Champagne and Carole Goldberg University of Arizona Press,
2021

*A COALITION OF LINEAGES: The Fernandeño Tataviam Band of Mission Indians* is a
timely narrative that weaves together the history of California with mission records, oral history interviews, documents, newspaper clippings, and
personal photographs to document the lineage of the Fernandeño Tataviam
Band of Mission Indians (FTBMI). Beginning in 2007, in collaboration with
the tribe, this book offers insights into the approach of researchers involved
in the FTBMI's federal recognition petition. *A Coalition of Lineages* tackles
two main objectives. First, the authors document and place the tribe in the
temporal narrative of the United States and California. Second, Champagne
and Goldberg use theoretical and methodological approaches to document
the continuity of the FTBMI into the twenty-first century, a requirement of
the federal recognition process.

Champagne and Goldberg carefully guide readers across seven chapters to
reinscribe the FTBMI in relation to preinvasion, the Spanish missionization,
Mexican authority, and eventually the U.S. Chapter 1, "Cultures and Communities Before the Mission (pre-1797)," draws from ethnographic material
to discuss the tribe's sociopolitical order and cultural practices predating
the establishment of the Spanish mission system in California in 1769. The
authors discuss geographic locations of villages, religious practices across
lineages, social organization between village lineages, political leadership,
economy, and spiritual practices including ceremonies, many of which are
shared with the Gabrielino to the south and Chumash in the north. Chapter
2, "Lineages Within Spanish Colonization (1797–1821)," addresses adaptations to social and political organization in response to the Spanish mission
system, specifically the establishment of the San Fernando mission in 1797.
Comparatively, chapter 3, "Continuity and Dispossession (1821–1850),"
outlines adaptations by the tribe under Mexican governance between 1821
and 1850, specifically focusing on the secularization of the Spanish mission
system and its implications on the distribution of lands to settlers. Chapter
4, "Statehood to Eviction (1850–1885)," focuses on the especially corrosive
implications of U.S. federal practices and California state policies, including
the failed treaty making process between 1851 and 1852 and the complex

land claims process, both of which strategically dispossessed the tribe from their lands. The final chapters focus on the efforts of tribal descendants to maintain their lineal connections and their deliberate efforts to collectively organize as a coalition. In situating the FTBMI in the broader historical narrative of the U.S. and California, the authors draw into focus how the tribe was dispossessed from their lands through coercion in the form of unethical and complex land allocation practices and claims processes across three colonial empires. This approach cleverly situates the argument for federal recognition around land dispossession.

Champagne and Goldberg also use theoretical and methodological approaches to explicate the FTBMI continuity across three dispossessions. First, the authors highlight the traditional social order of the FTBMI, pointing out that the tribe has always had a decentralized organization, where their political model evolved around individual villages. Thereafter, they apply social theory in identifying how the members of this coalition intentionally engaged change, resistance, and inclusion in their culture, government, social order, and economy as a *response* to dispossessions. While federal policies and practices and California state policies had consequential impacts on the tribe, this reframing draws into focus the agency and tenacity of descendants as they adapt to new conditions and maintain connections to their lands and each other into the twenty-first century and reject victimization and erasure. To this end, the authors aptly demonstrate how the FTBMI sustained sociopolitical continuity despite violent circumstances. Methodologically speaking, a compelling aspect of *A Coalition of Lineages* is the approach taken by the authors to trace the coalition of the FTBMI through the entire book. Across all chapters, the accounts of three lineages—Ortega, Ortiz, and Garcia—provide unifying threads at each point of dispossession. This genealogical practice reflects commonplace oral traditions of Indigenous Peoples; namely passing on family histories orally. *A Coalition of Lineages* proves to be an invaluable example for unrecognized Native nations seeking federal acknowledgment.

Finally, and somewhat unrelated to the intentions of the book, *A Coalition of Lineages* is a thoughtful tribute to the late Rudy Ortega Sr., who sustained the sociopolitical networks of FTBMI, served as their leader since the 1940s, and began the fight for federal recognition. The book also honors the ancestors who endured attempts by Spanish, Mexican, and U.S. governments to erase the tribe. This collaborative and community-engaged approach to research certainly proves to be an important contribution to Native American and Indigenous studies but, more impactfully, memorializes the FTBMI in the history of California.

THERESA STEWART-AMBO is assistant professor in education studies at the University of California—San Diego.

# ADAM W. COON

*Indigenous Peoples Rise Up: The Global Ascendency of Social Media Activism*
edited by Bronwyn Carlson and Jeff Berglund
Routledge, 2021

**INDIGENOUS PEOPLES RISE UP** offers a much-needed global exploration of Native activism on social media, addressing Indigenous movements principally within Australia, Aotearoa (New Zealand), and Northern Abiayala (U.S. and Canada). This collection analyzes myriad strategies to garner support, such as the deployment of memes, hashtags, and tweets. Taken together, the fourteen chapters underscore the far-reaching influence of Native artists and activists within online media.

The first essays focus on how movements have garnered support through hashtags and Facebook groups. In chapter 1, Alex Wilson and Corals Zheng examine the exponential growth of the Idle No More Movement (INM) through the hashtag #IdleNoMore. While they highlight the powerful role of social media, they also caution against the risks of large corporations' "free sites." The apprehension that participation on these sites could "end up funding our own domination" is a concern shared throughout *Indigenous Peoples Rise Up* (25). Nicholet A. Deschine Parkhurst posits that social media use in the #NoDAPL Movement disrupted existing colonial systems and created enduring connections. Bronwyn Carlson and Ryan Frazer observe how Native activists deploy anger and hope in posts tagged with #SOSBlakAustralia and #IndigenousDads to counter colonizing misrepresentations in Australia. Steve Elers, Phoebe Elers, and Mohan Dutta study how Māori #ThisIsNZ tweets rejected dominant narratives that depicted the 2019 Christchurch attacks as "unprecedented," a false portrayal that erases colonial violence (71). In chapter 5, Mounia Mnouer considers Amazigh Facebook groups that educate people about Amazigh and demand protection of their rights.

Subsequent chapters foreground Native LGBTIQ+ and women's innovations within social media. In chapter 6, Marisa Elena Duarte and Morgan Vigil-Hayes emphasize a "relational scholarship" that perceives the "interrelatedness of Indigenous science, technology, activism, and gender and belonging in digital studies," calling for consultation with Native domain experts to identify the issues that matter most to Native peoples (94). Taima Moeke-Pickering, Julia Rowat, Sheila Cote-Meek, and Ann Pegoraro study how Indigenous activism on Twitter amplifies women's voices on mainstream media in the movement for Missing and Murdered Indigenous Women and Girls (#MMIWG). Cutcha

Risling Baldy frames Indigenous women's social media activism in a "radical relationality" where new relatives are continually found struggling for territorial rights and systemic change (137). In chapter 9, Andrew Farrell explores how Aboriginal and Torres Strait Islander LGBTIQ+ activists engage in a "digital re-storying" that promotes justice and well-being through the Facebook group Black Rainbow (148).

The final chapters address Native artistic production and activism through social media. In chapter 10, Miranda Belarde-Lewis argues that art plays a fundamental role in advancing the work of social justice through an Indigenous lens. Jeff Berglund interviews Debbie Reese, whose blog, *American Indians in Children's Literature,* promotes works that accurately represent Native Nations. The blog format allows her to reference previous posts and openly acknowledge her own mistakes. Tristan Kennedy examines how Indigenous metal bands bypass traditional music production and directly share their perspectives through social media. Bronwyn Carlson interviews Dulguburra Yidinji media influencer Carly Wallace. Most known for her Facebook page "Cjay's Vines," Wallace humorously tells stories to expose and change stereotypes about Native peoples. In chapter fourteen, Jeff Berglund considers the influence of the 1491s, an Indigenous comedy troupe. Avoiding common depictions of Native peoples mired in "poverty porn," their YouTube videos highlight the "beauty, intelligence, survival and wit" of contemporary Native peoples in an "aesthetic activism" (218).

Authors throughout *Indigenous People Rise Up* foreground the need to build community not only within social media but also offline. They frame social media precisely as a tool to bring people into offline movements, privilege Native community building, promote empathy, and hold leadership accountable. Edited volumes like *Indigenous Peoples Rise Up* offer a key international approach to exploring Indigenous social media use. With that in mind, this volume could be strengthened by engagement with perspectives from Southern Abiayala (Latin America). In part because of language barriers, there is a tendency to do comparative studies that omit Native Nations south of the U.S.-Mexico border. For future studies, it would be ideal to have trans-Indigenous dialogues across Abiayala as a whole.

*Indigenous Peoples Rise Up* is a must-read for anyone studying Native online strategies. Analysis of Native social media use is an emerging field, and this volume helps lay the groundwork for ethical frameworks for analyzing this media. This text serves as a model for future studies of activism on (and off) social media.

ADAM W. COON is associate professor of Spanish and Latin American studies at the University of Minnesota, Morris.

# MOLLY McGLENNEN

*Ancestral Demon of a Grieving Bride*
by Sy Hoahwah
University of New Mexico Press, 2021

ANCESTRAL DEMON OF A GRIEVING BRIDE is a thrilling book of poems by enrolled member of the Comanche Nation of Oklahoma Sy Hoahwah. In the book's back matter, Ojibwe poet Heid Erdrich muses that Hoahwah "has perhaps invented Comanche goth," and I would have to agree—as skeletons rattle and serpents slither throughout the collection in haunting ways. But even this simile might be too limiting, as Hoahwah's poems deftly defy neat categories and metaphorical allusions. *Ancestral Demon*, in many ways, meditates on the act of mourning and memorialization. What is mourned is inherited. The substance of memory is the conjurer's trappings. "Oh ancestral demon," Hoahwah writes, "may my lamentation become verbal sorcery" (12).

Gothic allusions are not just referenced, however; Hoahwah mines them to expand a poetic world built from a multiplicity of myths, personal history, and Indigenous tribalographies. In it, we find bloody rivers, corpses, hexes, fangs, sacrifices, and something called a "raccoon-witch-cannibal-monk" (31). Viscera and decay preoccupy many poems, but this is not to suggest that there are only visceral connotations being made. Hoahwah's collection is also prophetic: "Birds don't fly here, / but there is the sound of wings. / . . . I carry sad omens" (28). Throughout, one follows a poetic map on Comanche terms, a map where night journeys and dreams orient the reader, even while eerie revenants creep up from behind: "Upwind, a tomb of antlers / asked my shadow for its hide / to lay a needle on its groove, / to hear its music" (18). Inscribing this complicated topography, Hoahwoah's poems embrace a landscape known and loved, one that is also marked by violence and loss. In his poem "It's Been 145 Years; I Am Still Surrendering to Ft. Sill," Hoahwoah writes,

> The Quohada went one way, the Kiowa another.
> The Cheyenne even another way.
> We're all cutting off fingertips, leaving trails of direction.
> The moon is the body and the funeral (9).

In one of his most poignant poems, one dedicated to Charles Simic, Hoahwah channels the starkness of the Yugoslavian poet-émigré to illuminate the embodied and residual effects of displacement. Via poetic cartography, Hoahwah guides the reader toward the hauntings of surrender, and of survival:

> We've all been chased to this genocidal beauty once or twice,
> Surrendering at a fast-food table with free Wi-Fi. . . .
> We're unable to tell the difference
> between the glow of smart maps
> and campfires of all who are closing in
> with ATM cards and 4G in hand.

For Hoahwah, personal and ancestral history, inheritance, and epigenetic trauma reside in the very body itself, the one that speaks aloud in his poems, and the one that proclaims at the end of "It's Been 145 Years" that "there is no sanctuary in the subdivisions we edge closer to / with our bowstrings cut" (9). In what might otherwise be characterized as yielding, Hoahwah's poems seek to challenge confident Western worldviews through which neat binaries can be chopped to pieces.

Throughout the collection, Hoahwah makes generous offerings despite "What is Left" (29) and despite the "Last Comanche Allotment at the Edge of the World" (26), saying "I am the cutoff, / the stump" (24), asserting that "I carve my name / on the moon's teeth" (29). The collection is filled with gestures such as these that deconstruct the normative categories that erect settler colonial power over Indigenous lands and bodies. "The offerings," Hoahwah says, "—dead spiders, hummingbirds, / and crispy sun-soaked leaves raked out of cemetery lawns," (24) become the altars for mourning and memorialization but also for the potential for immense beauty and connection. Perhaps in this Comanche gothic poetics, the miraculous survival is the "butterflies released by the breath of a vampire" (47), the way Indigenous collective memory holds to the lands and its people, the way one remembers and protects Indigenous patrimony, foiling the dreams of archaeologists.

Throughout his profoundly imaginative collection, Hoahwah illustrates the fallout from terror from his own Indigenous perspective, the way families and nations—reeling and breaking from loss—fervently find their ways around and through it. His poems, with their attention to craft, harness that devotion to access all of the "deepest part[s] of the world" (28). And for that, Sy Hoahwah's collection will haunt you well after you put the book down.

MOLLY MCGLENNEN is professor of English and Native American studies at Vassar College.

# DAVID H. DEJONG

*Where the Red-Winged Blackbirds Sing: The Akimel O'odham and Cycles
    of Agricultural Transformation in the Phoenix Basin*
by Jennifer Bess
University Press of Colorado, 2021

**JENNIFER BESS** adopts an Akimel O'otham—centric view of what is a tragic time
in the Gila River Indian Community's water history.[1] The Pima (Akimel
O'otham) were extraordinary growers until late nineteenth-century diversions deprived them of water. Bess begins with the Pima's story of their relationship to their land in the Gila River basin. She uses this to describe how
Pima core values resonated throughout their history and how their agricultural economy shaped and was shaped by trials and opportunities.

In *Where the Red-Winged Blackbirds Sing,* Bess demonstrates Pima resiliency and agency are nested in their conception of a worldview shaped by
their sacred "homelands and the fundamental values of adaptation, innovation, and co-creation" (17). This makes for refreshing reading. The narrative
begins not through the heuristic of Euro-American interactions but through
the lens of Pima story as informed by their Huhugam ancestors. The story is
neither interpreted through the lens of the historian nor through that of the
anthropologist but rather through a place-based framework that analyzes a
transformative era in Pima history. This peoplehood matrix enables Bess to
view Pima agency despite the theft of their water.

In seven chapters and with an ever-present Akimel O'otham voice and
examples of adaptation and cocreation, Bess illustrates that the Pima not
only survived and adapted to the exploitation of their natural and human
resources but they also engaged in "cultural continuity and economic transformation" (13). The fulcrum upon which their survival depended was their
"geographic stability in this desert oasis" (13). Notwithstanding years of
starvation, "dramatic change did not overwhelm" the Akimel O'otham
because they remained rooted in their *himdag,* which not only served as a
noun reflecting a way of life but also as a verb demonstrating their ability to
walk through life (125).

Chapter 1 sets the stage through the concept of how the Pima created a
worldview shaped by a shared history, culture, story, and place. This *himdag*
was rooted in security and prosperity and acted as an agent of strength and
resiliency in an agricultural-based place where all was sacred (30). Chapter

2 introduces adaptations introduced by Spanish technologies. Economic expansion and enhanced material culture resulted as the Pima interpreted what was compatible with their *himdag.* Chapter 3 continues the adaptation with the arrival of the United States and new technologies and markets that fueled the golden age of Pima agriculture (1850–1875).

The heart of the story begins in chapter 4 with the collapse of the Pima economy as a result of upstream diversions from brush dams that began in earnest in the early 1870s and devastated Pima crops by the late 1880s. While "the red-winged blackbirds [once] would sing" along the river, the lifeblood of the Pima now became "an empty bed full of sand" (93). The economic and environmental transformation of the Pima homeland was further influenced by federal policy bent on undermining traditional ways and knowledge and merging the people into the economic fringes of the expanding local market economy.

The final chapters focus on how federal policy appropriated the human and economic resources of the Pima, including the Bureau of Plant Industry's Sacaton experimental station and seed farm where researchers developed a new strain of Egyptian (Pima) cotton. This both enhanced resiliency and further marginalized tribal growers. Lacking water, the Pima were largely excluded from the local economic bonanza, becoming a source of cheap labor. Bess then hastens through the post-WWI development of the San Carlos Irrigation Project, although she fails to describe the integral role the Akimel O'otham played in securing passage of the bill.

While Bess tells an important story, she roots her analysis in a theoretical humanist framework that at times detracts from the story. However, she puts the Akimel O'otham and their culture, institutions, sacred places, and worldviews front and center. This is refreshing and represents the real strength of the story.

DAVID H. DEJONG is the director of the Pima-Maricopa Irrigation Project on the Gila River Indian Reservation. He has spent thirty-five years writing on and experiencing Pima agricultural and water rights history.

## Note

1. Bess uses the spelling Akimel O'odham while I use the commonly accepted spelling Akimel O'otham used by the Gila River Indian Community.

# KRISTINA ACKLEY

*Recasting the Vote: How Women of Color Transformed
    the Suffrage Movement*
by Cathleen D. Cahill
University of North Carolina Press, 2020

RECENT NATIONAL AND STATE DEBATES about ballot access reflect long-standing conflicts between expansive and limited views of suffrage. The centennial of
the Nineteenth Amendment in 2020 commemorated the women who fought
for their right to vote, but many of the public narratives contributed to a
narrow view that excluded women of color or relegated them to the background. Race was often presented as a binary. In contrast, Cahill foregrounds the work and words of a diverse group of activists of color in this
exemplary study, complicating the story of the Nineteenth Amendment and
voting rights more generally.

Cahill focuses on six women: Gertrude Simmons Bonnin (Yankton
Dakota), Mabel Ping-Hua Lee (Chinese-American), Carrie Williams Clifford
(African American), Marie Louise Bottineau Baldwin (Turtle Mountain Chippewa), Adelina "Nina" Luna Otero-Warren (Hispanic American), and Laura
Cornelius Kellogg (Oneida). Constructing the book chronologically in four
parts, each chapter is largely devoted to a few figures, leading to multiple
well-researched and impressively comprehensive narratives of the activists, illustrating how their motivations and experiences fueled their unique
contributions to the suffrage movement. Though their participation was
discouraged by some of the white women who led the national organizations, these activists refused to be left out.

Rather than limiting the definition of suffrage to white womanhood,
women of color insisted on demands for democratic rights and full citizenship. Cahill analyzes the richness and differences within the contexts of
place and region specifically and perceptively links debates about citizenship to suffrage, sovereignty, and land rights while contrasting immigrant,
Indigenous, and racialized experiences. Lee, an immigrant from China who
was barred from citizenship and voting through anti-Chinese legislation,
worked tirelessly to combat both anti-Chinese and gender discrimination.
Otero-Warren, whose family had resided on their lands long before the
region was recognized as the state of New Mexico, was a member of a family of political elites and held statewide office. Bonnin, Bottineau Baldwin,

and Cornelius Kellogg continually balanced the call for suffrage with advocacy to safeguard Indigenous sovereignty and land rights. Williams Clifford could not afford the luxury of privileging gender over race while she lived in a country that condoned lynchings and segregation, so she called for a reckoning with the violence that continued to be directed toward black bodies. For all these suffragists, race and political status were inextricable considerations of feminism.

With a careful attention to place and temporality, Cahill adds nuance to the narratives, tracing the changes in the priorities and movements of the women over time. In a discussion of Bonnin and Bottineau Baldwin, for example, Cahill examines how competing views of Indigenous citizenship and the focus of Washington, D.C. as the central place for Indigenous activism and intellectuals was contrasted with an emphasis on reservation communities. The interplay between reservation and city spaces continued to inform the political consciousness of Bonnin, Bottineau Baldwin, as well as Cornelius Kellogg, and directed their work in the following decades.

Cahill demonstrates the ways that the women's suffrage movement was transformed by "women who demanded their democratic rights as Americans while also fighting for equality as women of color" (3). Most of the women included did not leave formal archives or published sources, so Cahill impressively mines newspaper accounts, personal correspondence, speeches, and unpublished writings to document feminists of color challenges to the status quo. They rose to the occasion and fought for their own agendas, or what Clifford called "taking control of our own destinies in place of leaving them in the hands of white friends" (225).

Extending suffrage to women did not decisively ensure full voting rights for all, as access continued (and continues) to be a concern. But, as Cahill argues, the activists of color decisively changed the suffrage movement. These stories are a testament to the labor of suffragists of color and their efforts to create their own records through writing, advocating for legislation, a willingness to be in the media, and telling their stories to those who would make sure to bring them forward. Cahill rightly notes that contemporary readers should be indignant that this knowledge has been previously ignored or suppressed but also concludes that the real story is about "who remembered them and who saved their stories" (278). This book is an important step in recovering those voices, leading to a more comprehensive view of suffrage, and illuminating the genealogy of the movement for a broader definition of feminism.

KRISTINA ACKLEY is member of the faculty in Native American and Indigenous studies at The Evergreen State College.

# MELANIE BRAITH

*The Theatre of Regret*
by David Gaertner
University of British Columbia Press, 2020

DAVID GAERTNER'S *The Theatre of Regret* provides an in-depth critique of the concept of *reconciliation* and corresponding practices in the context of Canada's residential schools, the Truth and Reconciliation Commission (TRC), and ongoing settler colonialism. Gaertner, an assistant professor in the Institute of Critical Indigenous Studies at the University of British Columbia, writes as a settler scholar who criticizes settler colonial structures and unmasks their insidious, contemporary mechanisms. One argument at the heart of this monograph is that in Canada, "reconciliation has been recaptured by colonialism" (5). However, demonstrating how colonialism has coopted reconciliation is only half of the work that Gaertner sets out to do.

*The Theatre of Regret* also inspires its readers to think about what alternative conceptualizations of reconciliation could look like. As a settler scholar, Gaertner is careful not to take up too much space in this discussion as he finds it "imperative that we insist on a reconciliation that centres Indigenous perspectives and creates space for Indigenous voices by quieting settler colonial attempts to define the work" (227). Hence, Gaertner's methodology is related to what Métis scholar Judi Iseke defines as "pedagogical witnessing" (10), and for Gaertner, witnessing is an act that is "generated in the reciprocal act of listening to and sharing stories and the active deconstruction of settler colonial narratives" (10). Part of this methodology is to create space to amplify Indigenous voices. Therefore, *The Theatre of Regret* listens to Indigenous art and literature to learn how they imagine reconciliation.

A significant strength of Gaertner's work is that he embeds his critique of reconciliation in settler colonial Canada within a thorough discussion of the concept's international history. Gaertner examines the Nuremberg trials and TRCs that have occurred in Uganda, Chile, Australia, and South Africa. Scholarly work that compares the TRC in Canada to South Africa's TRC from 1995 to 2002 has been published in the past, and Gaertner, like others before him, points out that Canada (as opposed to South Africa) is a country where a Truth and Reconciliation Commission occurred without political transition. This fact forms a basis for Gaertner's analyses, and the book's title refers to reconciliation practices in which "concrete political transition is never a part of the terms of conversation" (51). In the theatre of regret, "reconciliation is founded on the promise of change and performances that convince the audience that while the government remains structurally and ideologically unchanged, it will now *act* differently" (51). Gaertner's analyses demonstrate how and where the theatre of regret is at work in Canada. He is, however, careful not to discard the work of residential school survivors, and he makes sure to acknowledge that the TRC is "a judicially determined survivor initiative" and not "a government instrument" even though many Canadians still believe it to be the latter (225).

The book's four chapters are arranged according to "four of the key stages on the path to reconciliation: acknowledgement, apology, redress, and forgiveness" (16). In each chapter, Gaertner analyzes one key concept and how it has been enacted within the framework of reconciliation in Canada. Then he performs compelling literary analyses that illustrate how Indigenous artists and writers conceive of the concept under discussion. For example, Gaertner analyzes Cherokee and Greek author Thomas King's parody of the apology industry in *Green Grass, Running Water* together with Métis playwright Marie Clemens's *Burning Vision* and its character Rose's angry monologue on hollow apologies in Canadian contexts. Gaertner contrasts these texts with former conservative Prime Minister Stephen Harper's apology to residential school survivors. Other writers that are analyzed at length include Nlaka'pamux playwright Kevin Loring, Anishinaabe author Richard Wagamese, Haisla and Heiltsuk author Eden Robinson, and Métis author Cherie Dimaline. When discussing the concept of forgiveness, Gaertner engages with the work of Japanese internment survivor Joy Kogawa—a discussion that fits well with the book's analysis of redress that takes the Japanese Canadian Redress Agreement into account when discussing redress for residential school survivors.

Published five years after the TRC's closing ceremony, *The Theatre of Regret* offers a thought-provoking critique of "reconciliation" as it has been captured by settler colonialism. Gaertner's strong analyses of Indigenous literary works and art help to demonstrate the work that Indigenous writers and artists do to imagine reconciliation differently.

**MELANIE BRAITH** is the project manager of the Six Seasons of the Asiniskaw Īthiniwak project at the University of Winnipeg. She holds a Ph.D. in Indigenous literatures; her research focuses on Indigenous oral storytelling.

# LAURA E. FORSYTHE

*Daniels v. Canada: In and Beyond the Courts*
edited by Nathalie Kermoal and Chris Andersen
University of Manitoba Press, 2021

**DANIELS V. CANADA:** *In and Beyond the Courts* explores the Pandora's box opened by the Supreme Court of Canada (SCC) decision that positioned "Métis-as-mixed"; the editors and authors ask the reader to consider the myriad complex issues that arose in its wake. After seventeen years of litigation, the SCC determined in *Daniels v. Canada* (2016) that Métis and Non-Status Indians were covered under s.91(24) of the Constitution Act, 1867. Section 91(24) states that the federal government has exclusive authority over Indians. The victory established the locus of responsibility for the Métis and at least theoretically ended the game of jurisdictional avoidance long played by the provincial and federal levels of government. The edited collection speaks to the decisions affecting Métis people's history, genealogy, identity, law, and genomics while debating policy ramifications and legal outcomes.

Part 1, "History," the first section of the collection, outlines the history and lived experience of Métis after the Second World War, a time when they were ignored by all levels of government despite their need for programs and services. Tony Belcourt, who was instrumental in bringing the case to the courts, recounts his life as a Métis growing up in this era to frame the conditions of governmental neglect. Nathalie Kermoal examines how the social and political circumstances of the 1970s and 1980s motivated Harry Daniels to pursue s. 91(24) recognition. Both chapters provide a basis for understanding the struggle to have the case heard in the nation's highest court.

In Part 2, "Legal Analyses," the collection moves to legal analyses of the decision. Jason Madden compares the *Daniels* decision to a Rorschach inkblot test "because everyone who reads it will see what they want within it" (44). His chapter provides the Métis Nation perspective as seen through his time preparing litigation as the legal counsel of the Métis Nation of Alberta and a Métis citizen. The court decision and the implications of Madden's claims caused hysteria. Arend J. A. Hoekstra and Thomas Isaac claim that *Daniels* constitutes a shift in judicial language by introducing the word "Indigenous" into law while highlighting the introduction of a new framework for

s. 91(24) that contrasts with the framework of s. 35 of the Constitution Act, 1982. Catherine Bell focuses on the last two declarations of the judgment, which the court denied, charging the SCC with creating confusion about the responsibilities of the Crown regarding the "fiduciary relationship" and "context-specific duty" to "negotiate" with Indigenous Peoples. This argument is followed by D'Arcy Vermette's assertion that, regardless of the victory of acknowledging federal responsibility for Métis, a review of SCC decisions demonstrates that their determinations are functionally racist in terms of Métis identity. Finally, Brenda L. Gunn tackles the implications of the decision from an international law perspective, especially regarding the United Nations Declaration on the Rights of Indigenous Peoples and the uprising of self-declared Métis people claiming Indigenous identity seeking to benefit from the court's decision. Overall, this section strives to raise awareness of the many complications brought on by the jargon and indecisiveness in *Daniels*.

The remaining essays in Part 3, "Societal Implications," consider the fallout and broader societal implications of the decision on who claims victory and who has begun to claim Métis identity. First, Chris Andersen seeks to unpack the decision's various strands of logic while exposing the differing interpretations that Indigenous political organizations have used to claim victory, followed by a chapter in which Rick W. A. Smith, Lauren Springs, Austin W. Reynolds, and Deborah A. Bolnick introduce the problematic—and dangerous—concept of genomics in producing and proclaiming notions of belonging. Darryl Leroux emphasizes the concerning practice of claiming Métis identity by using a relative from the 1600s as the sole basis for connection. Finally, Brenda Macdougall addresses the limitations of genealogical research that allow those with distant connections to imagine a new identity.

The collection both clarifies and muddies the understanding of *Daniels v. Canada*, forcing the reader to consider all its ramifications. As a Métis citizen who cheered the decision alongside my family, friends, and nation, I am grateful for this collection, which reminds us all of the legal and societal implications that remained once the cheering stopped.

LAURA E. FORSYTHE is an assistant professor at the University of Winnipeg in the Faculty of Education.

# KATHRYN BUNN-MARCUSE

*Cataloguing Culture: Legacies of Colonialism in Museum Documentation*
by Hannah Turner
UBC Press, 2020

DATA IS NOT NEUTRAL. Hannah Turner's *Cataloguing Culture: Legacies of Colonialism in Museum Documentation* demonstrates how data is shaped by both the extraordinary aims and goals of key individuals in anthropology—specifically at the Smithsonian's National Museum of Natural History (NMNH)—and the mundane daily tasks of recording, inventorying, naming, describing, and reinscribing data associated with cultural heritage collections. We witness the small and large acts of bureaucracy that contribute to intellectual colonialism and its solidification in institutions. Turner asserts that "how" is a more interesting question than "why," thus each chapter leads the reader through how data was organized and the various generations of technologies that museums have used to keep track of and understand their collections. While Turner delves deep into the details, the examples she highlights illuminate how their effects persist to this day.

In the first chapters, we are reminded of the colonial attitudes of early ethnographic collectors whose field guides sanctioned and recruited the collection of Native American human remains, as well as cultural creations. Turner reveals how these cultural belongings ("objects") stood in for the cultures themselves and represented Native history for anthropologists whose Eurocentric belief was that without written accounts there was no "real" Indigenous history to be relied upon. These early chapters also demonstrate how Indigenous creations became "specimens" through the recording of data about them and how the original ledger book columns for particular kinds of data encoded the values of the scientists, anthropologists, and museum professionals, constraining what and whose knowledge could be recorded.

Turner delves into the key actors within the NMNH, including curators Otis Mason and William Sturtevant, demonstrating their impact on institutional structures. Mason's desire to have a card catalog as a "tool for creating a universal index of all human culture" (19) and Turner's examination of the quotidian work of data entry presents cataloging as a "performative knowledge process" in which biases get normalized, hiding the political nature of these actions (16). We see how early collections that included plants, animals, and human creations (as well ancestors themselves) were divided up into all the "ologies" of a natural history and culture museum, reflecting compartmentalization of the natural world not reflective of Indigenous ways of knowing. The organization of natural history collections and data shaped how cultural collections were sorted, enforcing Eurocentric classifications on them, and often erasing the Indigenous Peoples and their knowledge from these information infrastructures.

As a curator, reading this book revealed how so many of the systems, data structures, and even my own daily museum practices are directly shaped by decisions and practices put in place more than a century ago. Authority files, naming lexicons, accession records and their emphasis on donors, and the fields in our cultural heritage databases all have their origins in museums like the Smithsonian and through curators like Mason. Mason's racist theories on "primitive" cultures and the evolutionary trajectory of their material creations have long been rejected, but his organizational schemes are still very much in place. If museums want to be places of relationship and reconciliation, how can this be if we are still encased in organizational systems that were developed during times of intense colonial damage to Native communities?

The most compelling sections of the book are the case studies such as the belongings taken from the Tlingit community at Hoonah in 1884 by Lieutenant Bolles. Turner's unpacking of this collection and the terminology and organization imposed upon it demonstrate the direct impact on how communities today can be hindered by those practices. More case studies would have brought to life the impact of all the small and large decisions outlined in earlier chapters and could have made space for contemporary Indigenous voices telling of their own experiences in colonial institutions.

One of the key contributions of *Cataloguing Culture* is to lay bare the history of how data has been created in ways that can obscure and hinder current efforts at repatriation and reconciliation. Because museum records are often given weight as authoritative data under NAGPRA and even considered neutral data by some, this has real life impacts on communities who are working toward the repatriation of their cultural heritage. Turner's book lays out the histories that have led us to today. These histories must be understood as we work on reconciliation and the reunification of material cultural belongings with their communities.

KATHRYN BUNN-MARCUSE is associate professor of art history at the University of Washington and curator of Northwest Native Art at the Burke Museum.

# NO'U REVILLA

*Words Like Love*
by Tanaya Winder
University of New Mexico Press, 2021

**IN THE POEM** "when we banish tongues," the speaker asks the same question twice: Where are the books? Where are the books? By the time we arrive here in Tanaya Winder's collection *Words Like Love,* we can consider the toxic legacy of Indian boarding schools and the erasure of Indigenous wisdom by genocide and settler colonialism in order to begin answering the speaker's question. Yet by this poem we are also equipped to consider abundance. In *Words Like Love,* Winder testifies to many ways of archiving, transmitting, and reciting knowledge. Just as power is not bound to English or linear thinking, knowledge is not bound to books.

What about that which is simultaneous and unraveling, like braids or rivers?

What about the intergenerational surge of survival and compassion, even in the watery afterlife of grief?

Unsurprisingly, when imagining their descendants, the speaker of "when we banish tongues" declares a decolonial future:

> we will tell our children
> we needed the entire sky
> to tell our story (33)

Later, in section 3 of the book, another expansive approach to literacy is revealed.

In "the war on words," the speaker begins and ends with an image of a man and woman sharing poetry. While the first couplet depicts the pair reading poetry to each other, the final couplet depicts them writing poetry on each other's bodies:

> Somewhere a man
> and a woman write poetry to each other,
>
> he writes *remembering* on her outer thigh. She writes
> *history* on his chest. They write until no empty space is left. (48)

People find and choose each other in this collection. They are directed, as we are, by a resilient and generous (at times shattering) desire for connection:

"to know what it was like to touch each other" (6). Winder's gaze settles on more than the beginnings and breaks of romantic love. She also pieces together fragments of friendship, genealogy, and origin stories, explaining: "We try to go back to our beginnings // fill in the disconnections and blanks" (66).

Although bell hooks was right—suffering does not sanctify—our lived experiences are knowledge, and Winder is thoughtful and honest about how "our brokenness / navigates like a compass" (49). How can we become good ancestors if we deny the intergenerational effects of settler colonialism? How can we become good ancestors if we refuse to center the ways we choose to heal and take care of each other? How do we cultivate the energy to keep asking questions of our histories so that we may stand in our bodies and on our lands, sovereign and unafraid?

Many of these questions are tested against the "slurred performance" of containment and denial (30). Importantly, Winder goes beyond the mere presentation of trauma in order to feel something despite / because of / alongside / within / between grief and fear. A feeling body is a thinking body, after all.

In one of the most moving exchanges in the book, a young man courageously incorporates singing into his poem, specifically lyrics from Nina Simone's "Blackbird." The speaker of the poem is the young man's teacher. The poem "patrick would never say the word *love*" is one any Indigenous poet privileged to work with young writers can relate to. Across twelve stanzas, Winder illustrates how the risk and reward of rising in one's voice can ripple through a classroom.

"Performing his piece inspires the quiet," the teacher observes (54).

In *Words Like Love,* readers learn that silence is neither passive nor homogenous. Silence can be used to create or weaponized to condemn and destroy. So whose hands do we reach for? Whose hands, pooling with language, do we trust to nourish, protect, and guide us?

"Performing his piece inspires the quiet," the teacher observes.

And seeing him stand strong in his poem inspires another student to raise her hand and "rise into flight" (54). In *Words Like Love,* the motif of wings takes on ecstasy and loss, fragility and power, loneliness and the collective. *Words Like Love* is a chronicle of hope and invention despite / because of / alongside / within / between.

NOʻU REVILLA ʻŌIWI (Hawaiian) is assistant professor of creative writing at the University of Hawaiʻi-Mānoa.

# WENDY MAKOONS GENIUSZ

*Dadibaajim: Returning Home through Narrative*
by Helen Olsen Agger
University of Manitoba Press, 2021

THERE ARE FAR TOO MANY WONDERFUL THINGS to say about *Dadibaajim* in this short review. Focusing on the Namegosibii Trout Lake community (Ontario), Agger's text is a beautifully laid-out *miikaanens* (trail) that other Indigenous scholars could follow to write about their own communities and research. Agger provides instruction on important protocols for working with elders, which will be useful to a variety of audiences, especially those working in and with Indigenous communities and those working with previously collected *dadibaajim* narratives. Agger's text also warns about the problems of prior research, especially that done by outsiders, on Indigenous communities. These warnings can aid scholars from all backgrounds, as well as policymakers, who sincerely wish to work with Indigenous communities to create a decolonized, reconciled future.

The only warning I have for prospective readers of *Dadibaajim* is that it is an academic text, clearly written for academics. While that is a wonderful prospect for my colleagues hoping to find an invigorating text for their Indigenous research methodologies courses (yes, this is it!), I hope Agger writes another version of this text that is accessible to a wider audience. I also have one correction to make. The phrase "Gego zhaaganaashiiyaadizisiidaa" is not, as Agger states, a phrase used by the elders my mother worked with at Seven Generations Educational Institute. It is simply a title of a presentation I gave at *Anishinaabewin Niswi* (131). I was modifying the verbs: wemitigoozhiiwaadizi and zhaagnaashiiyaadizi, both of which that group of elders used and both of which refer to being colonized, living as a white person at the expense of being Anishinaabe.

Throughout her text, Agger advocates, quite eloquently, for Anishinaabemowin, Ojibwe, and other Indigenous languages and oral narratives: "It is important to keep in mind that effective forms of knowledge transmission existed long before Europeans imposed literatism. The text is a human construction, neither natural nor neutral" (63). She emphasizes the necessity of Indigenous language revitalization being a part of all decolonization efforts: "Use of English or other colonial languages perpetuates the domination of the wemitigoozhiiwaadiziwin way of thinking" (36). Agger's arguments make a compelling case for having substantial Indigenous language requirements as part of all Indigenous studies degrees; they are a rallying cry for those of us who can research and publish in our Indigenous languages to do so now, before we lose any more of our first-language speakers and before we are presented, yet again, to the world in words that are not our own and in languages that can, at best, only summarize key concepts of our philosophies.

Agger's text itself will contribute to language revitalization efforts. As a language learner and educator, I am grateful for the amount of space in this text that Agger and her editors dedicate to transcriptions of first-language Ojibwe speech. All too often, we only get translations of elders' words, rather than being able to read what they actually said in their languages. Agger shares an entire chapter of *dadibaajim* related to place names that had not been previously documented. This section contains invaluable material on teachings, fluency patterns, and information for other language and culture revitalization and research.

For several decades in Canada and the United States we have been going through a strong period of Indigenous cultural revitalization, in which some teachings have been embraced as "pan-Indian" or, more recently, "pan-Indigenous." When these teachings differ from those in a particular community, the older teachings are often replaced. I have seen this throughout my lifetime. Agger gives examples of how some of today's widely accepted pan-Indigenous teachings of are not part of traditional Namegosiibii Anishinaabe culture. She notes that Sweet Grass is "not a traditional component of Namegosiibii Anishinaabe cultural practice" (40). The concepts of Turtle Island and Mother Earth were not recognized by elders in her community (36). Her statements make a strong case for the importance of recording and retaining the diversity within our Indigenous communities, including the diversity between communities that speak the same language. To do otherwise is not decolonizing but creating yet another form of colonization.

For decades, outside researchers have superimposed categories and geographic groupings on Indigenous Peoples. Agger argues that these divisions have erased entire distinct communities and ignored important differences between neighboring communities. Through *Dadibaajim,* she speaks out against the attempted erasure of Namegosiibi, amplifies her elders' voices and language, acknowledges histories that have been ignored, and gives us all a new perspective on the healing process of decolonization.

**WENDY MAKOONS GENIUSZ** (Cree and Métis) is professor of sociology at York University.

# KATHLEEN S. FINE-DARE

*Coming Home to Nez Perce Country: The Niimíipuu Campaign
to Repatriate Their Exploited Heritage*
by Trevor James Bond
Washington State University Press, 2021

HISTORIAN TREVOR JAMES BOND has written a compelling and beautifully illustrated account of the successful efforts by the Niimíipuu (Nez Perce) People to regain—at a high price—cultural property taken from them in the mid-nineteenth century as part of a "civilizing" missionary project. The book's organization—which Bond aptly characterizes as a "life history of a collection"—is tripartite (8). Part 1, "Collecting" is an account of how the objects comprising what became known as the Spalding-Allen Collection traveled cross-country in barrels from the Columbia Plateau to Ohio. Part 2, "Away from Home," tells us more about the colonization history of the Niimíipuu People and the ways they later communicated with Ohio Historical Society (OHS) officials after the objects were found to be in OHS hands. The chapters in Part 3 are dedicated to "The Campaign" to raise enough funds (a "market price" of over $600,000) to buy back their own Niimíipuu heritage. By the end of the six-month purchase window in 1996 the Nez Perce Heritage Quest had raised the necessary sum from many sources, including schoolchildren's projects, grunge-band fundraisers, individual donors, and support expressed in *The Denver Post* and other media outlets. To raise awareness The Heritage Quest also created a website where individual items were displayed and their stories told—such as magnificent women's dresses and men's shirts, baskets, horse regalia, and a woman's saddle.

How and why these precious objects were taken is a sadly familiar story. In the case of missionary Henry Harmon Spalding, the objects he and his wife collected from the Nez Perce Tribe in the 1830s served two purposes. The first—accompanied by "harsh punishments" such as public whippings—was to suppress Niimíipuu culture, "including the wearing of regalia," and other practices so that the Nez Perce would become Christian sedentary farmers (18). The second purpose was to send to Ohio "Indian curiosities" desired by Henry's college buddy, Dudley Allen, in exchange for trade items needed by the mission to keep it financially afloat.

The remainder of the story entails mind-boggling communications, broken promises, and obscure exchanges between Oberlin College, the OHS, Case Western Reserve University, the Nez Perce National Historical Park, the Burke Museum, and a host of other individual and sometimes shady (and clueless) characters. Bond also describes other heartbreaking stories of objects and collections taken from the Niimíipuu and other Plateau Peoples, including Chief Joseph's famous beaded and quilled deer hide war shirt, first recorded in 1877 when the leader sat for a photo with frostbitten hands following a military rout and a four-hundred-mile forced march. After Chief Joseph's death in 1904 on the Colville Reservation, the shirt passed through many hands, reappearing in a 2012 Sotheby's sale in Reno where it was sold to an anonymous buyer for $877,500. The shirt is now believed to be locked up in one of the private mansions of billionaire William I. Koch (151–152).

Bond's narrative ends in the summer of 2021, when he participated in events marking the  twenty-fifth anniversary of the repatriation purchase. In a ceremony held on June 26, the collection was renamed *Wetxuuwíitin'*—"returned after a period of captivity." Shortly after *Coming Home to Nez Perce Country* was published, members of the Ohio History Connection (formerly the OHS) visited the Nez Perce reservation on November 23, 2021, to return the full payment of $608,100 to the People. Tribal Executive Committee Chairman Samuel Perry remarked in a statement made to Cassie Packard of *Hyperallergic* (published December 8, 2021):

> These healing steps—bringing the items home, providing a fitting name and now reimbursement—give our people hope and build on that connection that's been missing for far too long.

**KATHLEEN S. FINE-DARE** is professor emerita of anthropology and gender studies at Fort Lewis College in Durango, Colorado. She was formerly a faculty affiliate with the Native American and Indigenous Studies program and currently serves as the college NAGPRA compliance liaison.

# KELLY WISECUP

*Speaking for the People: Native Writing and the Question*
  *of Political Form*
by Mark Rifkin
Duke University Press, 2021

**SPEAKING FOR THE PEOPLE** focuses on four nineteenth-century Native American writers: Elias Boudinot (Cherokee), William Apess (Pequot), Sarah Winnemucca (Paiute), and Gertrude Bonnin/Zitkala-Ša (Yankton Dakota). Rifkin argues that these writers employed settler political forms, including treaties, conceptions of the nation and of hereditary leadership, and ethnographic genres, to access rhetorical platforms. These writers sought to define Indigenous Peoples in ways that would compel the U.S. to act differently toward Indigenous polities. Rifkin traces how the authors pursued these ends by making certain narratives about their communities legible to settler readers. Collectively, the chapters argue that such engagement with settler forms amounts to political "work" rather than functioning as a wholesale identification with the ideological content of those forms or, on the other hand, referencing tribal sovereignty itself as experienced and practiced across their communities (6). Rifkin traces how creating views of peoplehood acceptable to the U.S. could result in sidelining other decision-making processes, especially those belonging to Indigenous women and nonelite Indigenous Peoples.

Rifkin's attention to negotiations over political form engages two interrelated conversations in Indigenous studies. First, Rifkin seeks to correct prior NAIS scholarship that, he posits, has read Indigenous literatures as indexing what he calls "extratextual political formations" (16) or the "Indigenous real" (5). He argues that scholars have mistakenly read Native writers' experimentation with political forms as reflective of actual Indigenous politics, taking as too much of a given that Indigenous writing reflects already established Indigenous conceptions of sovereignty. Rifkin's primary object of critique here is Lisa Brooks's *The Common Pot* (2008), which emerges in *Speaking for the People* as insufficiently accounting for the effects of settler contexts on Native writing. Rifkin seeks to offer alternatives to analyses that read Native writing "as somewhat mimetically bearing [extratextual formations] in ways that can replace 'colonial fantasy' and instead, convey Indigenous realities that lie beyond state-sanctioned frames of reference" (9).

Second, Rifkin asks what readings of nineteenth-century Native writing might contribute to recent discussions about the politics of recognition. He demonstrates how nineteenth-century writing illuminates the multiple outcomes of engaging settler forms. For example, chapter 4's discussion of Gertrude Bonnin's representations of Yankton Dakota life shows how working with settler forms can expose their limits and redirect their logic. Taking up the literary and political forms of recognition does not automatically entail identification with them. As the coda suggests, these four Native writers offer a view of Indigenous Peoplehood as contested, negotiated, and undecided, ultimately framing refusal not as the "opposite of recognition" but a "complex and shifting set of negotiations" regarding "Indigenous governance" (222).

*Speaking for the People* usefully models one avenue for bringing together contemporary NAIS scholarship on recognition and nineteenth-century Native writing, in ways that mutually illuminate both. Yet I remain unconvinced that *The Common Pot* is the right object for Rifkin's critique of ethnographic reading, in no small part due to Brooks's own methodology of considering the diplomatic work that writing did among and within Indigenous communities as well as settler audiences (Rifkin's focus remains on texts initially prepared for non-Native readers). Some of my skepticism revolves around Rifkin's own method: he tends to draw on a limited set of quotations, sometimes from Brooks's chapter summaries rather than from the book sections that more fully articulate her argument, and in some cases overlooks later commentary that would trouble his reading (see especially Rifkin 150, 175, 223). I am also mindful that *The Common Pot* focuses on eighteenth-century texts (with the exception of Apess's *Indian Nullification*). As a result, while I know that this question runs counter to Rifkin's move to ask what reading nineteenth-century texts might teach us about contemporary struggles, I do wonder if it is worth attending to what is specific about the nineteenth century? Also, given that it is in Bonnin's early twentieth-century reconfiguration of ethnographic forms that Rifkin locates alternative outcomes for working with settler templates for recognition, I wonder why he does not find this same disidentification in the nineteenth-century texts under consideration? These questions indicate how *Speaking for the People* has generated a rich set of coordinates and queries for analyzing nineteenth-century Native writing, and Rifkin's readings model how these questions take us deep into nineteenth-century Native political discussions while resonating in contemporary NAIS scholarship.

KELLY WISECUP is professor of English at Northwestern University.

# ANDREW DENSON

*Race, Removal, and the Right to Remain: Migration and the Making of the United States*
by Samantha Seeley
University of North Carolina Press, 2021

IN *RACE, REMOVAL, AND THE RIGHT TO REMAIN*, historian Samantha Seeley explores the politics of migration and exclusion in the United States during the early national period. Focusing on the Upper South, Middle Atlantic, and Ohio River Valley, she examines a series of "removal projects," (10) in which state and federal governments sought variously to deport Indigenous Peoples, restrict the movement of free African Americans, and promote Black "colonization," the emigration of free African Americans away from the United States. Together, she argues, these projects formed crucial steps in how early American political leaders defined the new United States as a white republic, creating a nation in which race determined who could enjoy the benefits of citizenship and political participation.

In the literature on United States history, the term "removal" most often refers specifically to the Indian removal policy of the antebellum era. As Seeley notes, however, that policy was just one of many efforts by early American governments to exclude or expel nonwhites. Earlier, in the years immediately following the Revolution, American leaders tried to treat Native nations as conquered enemies, demanding vast cessions of territory from Great Britain's former allies, and they defined the rapid opening of new lands to white settlement as essential to the well-being of the republic. The deportation of Native Americans, Seeley writes, was a "founding project" of the new nation (56). The later removal policy, she suggests, represented a revival of those older principles, rather than a new turn in Indian affairs. During this same period, state governments sought to restrict the movement of free African Americans. States in the Upper South and Ohio River Valley tried to close their borders to free Black migration, and Virginia passed a law requiring newly freed African Americans to leave the state within a year of manumission. These laws, Seeley suggests, followed a racist logic similar to that of Native American removal. In both cases, American politicians defined the very presence of nonwhite communities as dangerous to the republic, while making whiteness a condition for enjoying freedom and citizenship.

That reasoning also informed white support for Black colonization, an idea that allowed white Americans to reconcile misgivings about slavery with a commitment to maintaining white supremacy.

As Seeley explains, the architects of these removal projects often employed the language of civilization and improvement. Colonization advocates argued that free African Americans could never advance while they remained in the United States, which they insisted would always prove a hostile environment for former slaves. Emigration, by contrast, would provide opportunities for Black improvement, while those participating in colonization would help to bring civilization to less advanced parts of the globe. That reasoning, Seeley observes, echoed the "humanitarian" argument for Indian removal, which held that Native Americans would not survive if they continued living alongside white communities within existing states. One of the great strengths of Seeley's work is the way in which she brings these different strains of early American racist thought into conversation with one another. Readers come to see these subjects, usually treated separately in the literature, as elements of the same process, in which white elites drew boundaries around belonging in the new republic.

In a similar fashion, Seeley draws together histories of Black and Native American resistance to these various removal projects. For example, she describes the multitribal unity movement that sought to prevent the United States from seizing the Ohio River country in the 1780s and 1790s and invites readers to compare that movement with growing Black opposition to colonization during the same period. Native and Black resistance took very different forms, but in both cases, critics of the new United States articulated a "right to remain" (3). In a particularly strong chapter, Seeley examines Black petitions requesting exemptions from the Virginia law requiring the newly manumitted to leave the state. These petitions, she suggests, represent a literature of freedom, in which African Americans explored the possibility of Black equality as they defended themselves against the threat of exile. Something similar can be said of Seeley's examples of Native and Black resistance more generally. In demanding the right to remain, Native Americans and free African Americans imagined alternatives to the white republic.

ANDREW DENSON is professor of history at Western Carolina University.

# LOUELLYN WHITE

*Did You See Us? Reunion, Remembrance, and Reclamation at an Urban Residential School*
by Survivors of the Assiniboia Indian Residential School, edited by Andrew Woolford
University of Manitoba Press, 2021

**WRITTEN BY SURVIVORS** of the Assiniboia Indian Residential School and edited by Andrew Woolford, this book is a refreshing read that highlights multiple perspectives of Assiniboia and is a testimony to the resilience of survivors. What is unusual is the inclusion of non-Indigenous contributors like school cook Sister Jean Ell, the school supervisor, local residents, and public-school teachers. I was apprehensive at first and sure non-Indigenous perspectives would detract from those who were so heavily impacted by residential schooling. However, led by the Assiniboia Indian Residential School (IRS) Legacy Group, the book is a result of annual reunions with survivors, school staff, and local residents; it stands as an effort toward reconciliation.

Located in Winnipeg, Assiniboia was unique as an urban Indian residential high school operating from 1958 to 1967 under the auspices of the Oblates of Mary Immaculate. From 1967 to 1973 Assiniboia served as a hostel where Indigenous youth stayed and were integrated into local high schools. The federal government ran the school from 1969 until its closing.

One story that resonates with the intention of the book as an act of remembrance and reconciliation is that of Theodore Fontaine, chief of Sagkeeng First Nation, and his non-Indigenous wife Morgan Sizeland-Fontaine. Sizeland-Fontaine recounts the time boys from the little-known "Indian School" came to shovel snow at her nearby home. Years later she worked with Fontaine at the Department of Indian Affairs, and they would later marry. It was not until several years had passed when they visited the former site of Assiniboia that they realized their childhood connection. Fontaine was one of the boys who knocked on her door to shovel snow all those years earlier. Sizeland-Fontaine writes: "We knew then that our relationship began at that door and that destiny had brought us together again in another doorway twenty years later" (157). The inclusion of non-Indigenous perceptions, interactions, and experiences like Fontaine's and Sister Jean Ell's—who maintained friendships with survivors over the years—contribute a more comprehensive picture of Assiniboia.

Perhaps surprisingly, many survivors recall their time at Assiniboia with fondness because they were treated with kindness and respect; participated in sports, music, art, and academic debates; and via school dances and integration with public schools during the hostel years, had a social life like they had never experienced before. They had plenty of food to eat, thanks to Sister Jean Ell, who treated them with a dignity unknown in the IRSs they had come from. Survivors recall a sense of freedom at Assiniboia, calling it an "oasis" (29) and the "best time in my life" (67).

However, the book cautions that Assiniboia should be measured against the often-painful experiences at other residential schools where abuse was rampant. Coming to Assiniboia was, as one survivor attests, like "peeking out of a dark place" (xx). Survivors came to Assiniboia during their high school years at an age when they were better able to care for themselves at a place that gave them hope.

Even though survivors generally paint a picture of Assiniboia with a rosier brush, it "was an experiment in keeping Indian children captive, while advancing toward the goals of assimilation and isolation from our Indian languages, culture, family and community" (16). There were rigid structures and rules and gender divisions. Stories do not reveal outward abuse, but one survivor says: "Abuse was not too invasive, but it was still there, only invisible" (78). Another was warned not to be alone with a certain priest, and one had intense flashbacks and negative feelings when she revisited the school. Teachers from local high schools remember Assiniboia students as passive, withdrawn, cautious, and mistrustful.

This book illustrates multiple perspectives and experiences that contribute to our understanding of the complexities of IRS. Fontaine states: "Engaging Assiniboia requires that we understand the variety of residential school experiences, while not using those that are on the surface positive, or at least not as outwardly violent as what has been captured in Truth and Reconciliation of Canada testimony and elsewhere to somehow absolve the system" (129).

Finally, the book reminds us that survivor stories belong to the survivors, regardless of where they fall on the vast, complex spectrum of IRS experiences. Although Assiniboia was "part of a system designed and enacted to destroy Indigenous identities, eliminate Indigenous Nations, and ensure the unquestioned dispossession of Indigenous territories" (129), for many, life-long friendships were made, and the lifeline that was Assiniboia continues to hold a special place in their memories.

LOUELLYN WHITE (Akwesasne Mohawk) is associate professor in the First Peoples Studies Program at Concordia University, Montreal.

# SIERRA WATT

*Voting in Indian Country: The View from the Trenches*
by Jean Reith Schroedel
University of Pennsylvania Press, 2020

JEAN REITH SCHROEDEL'S *Voting in Indian Country: The View from the Trenches* outlines the struggles experienced by Native Americans as they strive for full
participation in the American political process, both historically and in the
present day. Using mixed methods, including legal case history, voter turnout and registration data, survey data, case study, and oral history, Schroedel
lays out the landscape of Native voting rights and the continued existence of
voter suppression in tribal communities. The volume connects Native voting
rights case law with grassroots activism and voter mobilization efforts, setting it apart from other existing voting and civil rights scholarship.

Part 1 contextualizes United States citizenship for Native Americans and
the groups' current political status as tripartite citizens of their country,
state, and tribal nation. The section connects the activism among Native
communities, including the Red Power movement, the occupation of Alcatraz Island, and the water protectors at Standing Rock with the ongoing
fight for equitable access to the ballot box. Part 1 explains why Native Americans are considered a political minority group by the federal government
and their respective states and the way in which that status differentiates
them from the civil rights struggles of other racial and ethnic groups, while
still acknowledging shared experiences across groups, including disen-
franchisement, violent racism, and prejudice. Part 2 discusses more recent
attacks on Native voting rights, including state action to bar Native Americans who live on reservations from voting. The section focuses primarily
on a case study of Jackson County, South Dakota, utilizing voter turnout
and registration data to illustrate the way that non-Native voters are prioritized to the detriment of tribal citizens. Finally, Part 3, in contrast with
more traditional works of political science and legal studies, focuses on oral
histories of lawyers, activists, Native community members, and tribal politicians. This method grounds the work, making visible the experiences of
Native Americans in their continued uphill battle for equal voting rights.

Schroedel is at her best when tying contemporary legal struggles to the
real-life experiences of tribal communities. Connecting the challenges faced

by Native voters—including the "cracking" of Native districts to dilute their voting power; historical use of literacy tests to vote; language barriers for traditional language speakers; ongoing attacks on the use of tribal identification at the ballot box; extreme travel distances to cast a ballot on reservations; and restrictions on absentee and vote-by-mail—provides readers an understanding of the hardships faced on the ground. Her premise remains true today and in five of seven key battleground states that decided the outcome of the 2020 presidential election the size of the Native voting age population was larger than the margin of victory (Research Policy Update—Native Vote Report: 2020 Election Results. Washington DC: National Congress of American Indians Policy Research Center, December 10, 2020). This reality reifies her work: Native voters, despite small numbers, have the ability to impact election outcomes and thereby increase political representation for the needs of tribal communities.

Schroedel's work arrives at a time of increased surveillance and silencing for academics working on matters of equity and inclusion at the ballot box. The preface describes her path to this work and her legal testimony on behalf of Native voting rights in the *Wandering Medicine v. McCulloch* case. In a recent similar instance, the University of Florida attempted to bar three professors from testifying in a voting rights case. While the university ultimately reversed its decision, the message remains clear: academics' efforts to amplify the voices of the marginalized are under attack. Undeterred, Schroedel continues as an academic consultant for the Native American Voting Rights Coalition.

Few understand as Schroedel does that political repression continues in Indian Country. During the recent Senate Committee on Indian Affairs hearing, "Voting Matters in Native Communities," senators expressed disbelief that Natives still face these challenges of access to the ballot box. Their disbelief is proof that more work in this area is needed. As states develop new voting district lines based on the 2020 Census, Schroedel's volume and research work is more critical than ever. Her concise but in-depth book provides a thorough primer on Native American voting, which deserves to stand alongside key works on Native politics and voting rights.

SIERRA WATT (Pechanga Band of Luiseño) is a doctoral candidate at the University of Kansas and a research associate at the National Congress of American Indians.

# COURTNEY LEWIS

*A Drum in One Hand, a Sockeye in the Other*
by Charlotte Coté
University of Washington Press, 2022

*A DRUM IN ONE HAND, a Sockeye in the Other,* the most recent book by Charlotte Coté (Tseshaht/Nuu-chah-nulth; associate professor in American Indian studies at the University of Washington) continues her trend of exceptional scholarship that draws from her academic and personal expertise on the politics of food sovereignty for Indigenous Peoples in the Pacific Northwest. While *Spirits of Our Whaling Ancestors: Revitalizing Makah and Nuu-chah-nulth Traditions* (University of Washington Press, 2010) delved deeply into the complications of whaling reclamation efforts, *A Drum in One Hand* provides a broad exploration of the Indigenous food sovereignty movement as seen through the lens of Coté and her family's practices.

To open the preface, Coté introduces herself in the Nuu-chah-nulth language, an important moment that positions Coté and sets the tone for a work that will prioritize what it preaches: actions of active reclamation. *A Drum in One Hand* frequently incorporates the Nuu-chah-nulth language; while some authors may worry that this would dissuade non-Nuu-chah-nulth language readers (like myself), the use of this language provides a depth to the understanding of these food sovereignty issues that would not be in evidence otherwise. The introduction takes us through a day of *qaal-qaawi* (wild berry) picking, expertly interweaving the voices of Coté, her people, and academic sources while laying out her terminology (e.g., challenging terms such as "wild" for foods that are cultivated by Indigenous Peoples). This "methodology of storytelling" (7)—utilized to translate Indigenous knowledge, experience, and history—continues throughout the book. The introduction ends with an indictment of global industrial food systems' role in the creation of food insecurity, noting that "food insecurity for Indigenous Peoples goes beyond the current definition that focuses on monetary access to industrial foods" (16).

In chapter 1, the author delves deeply into the concept and practices of food sovereignty, starting on a global level and then narrowing the conversation to those specific to the Nuu-chah-nulth. Throughout, Coté provides examples of Indigenous initiatives and creative responses to settler-colonial incursions. The focus on restorative food justice in this chapter culminates in an update on her previous whaling work. Salmon is the focus of chapter 2, beginning with a discussion of settler-colonial disruptions of the land and potlaches, including anthropologists' roles in furthering misinformation about Northwest Coastal Indigenous Peoples. Fish Day is heavily documented here, including documentation of its current state and discussion regarding issues for sustaining this practice.

The reclamation of both Indigenous Peoples' and the land's wellness through community gardening is delicately woven with the continuing trauma of boarding schools in chapter 3 by detailing the location of the Tseshaht Community Garden on the Alberni Indian Residential School site. Many horrors of these schools are recounted, including unethical multiyear food-deficiency experiments on children. Coté also follows some community members' initial disinterest in the garden as well as what it means for the community to reclaim their health through fresh, whole foods.

Chapter 4 helps to address the question of what it actually takes for one family to reclaim their foodways. Coté follows kamåmakskwew, waakiituusiis Nitanis Desjarlais, and riaas?atuk John Rampanen as they move their nuclear family to a remote Vancouver island with the intention of decolonizing their diets and their lives. They resided there for ten months, through times both beautiful and terrifying, but ultimately returned to regain what they lacked on Seitcher Bay: community. Finally, the epilogue provides a contextualization of the book's topics during the COVID-19 pandemic, centering its impact and the agency of Indigenous Peoples as they navigate this most recent threat to their health and lives.

Coté's robust transdisciplinary engagement with existing Indigenous food studies research will make this a useful book for scholars who want to delve more deeply into this literature, while her engaging personal stories and clear writing style also allow its use in both undergraduate and graduate classes. When read alongside *Indigenous Food Sovereignty in the United States* (Mihesuah and Hoover, University of Oklahoma Press, 2019), readers will come away with a foundational knowledge of the current state of North American Indigenous food sovereignty research and practices.

COURTNEY LEWIS (Cherokee Nation citizen) is associate professor of anthropology and the Institute for Southern Studies at the University of South Carolina.

# BRANDON CASTLE

*Unsettling Native Art Histories on the Northwest Coast*
edited by Kathryn Bunn-Marcuse and Aldona Jonaitis
University of Washington Press, 2020

**AN INCREDIBLE VOLUME** of Northwest Coast scholarship, art-historical analysis, Indigenous knowledge, and a confluence of literary power linked together through intergenerational visioning, *Unsettling Native Art Histories on the Northwest Coast* signals a change in how Indigenous art is contextualized both academically and institutionally. By questioning the foundations of subjects like art history, museology, and Northwest Coast scholarship, previous definitions and categorizations of Indigenous art are pushed outside of stifling boundaries. In a collaborative effort, the long-held biases surrounding Native Northwest Coast art are carefully examined against the multiplicity of histories impacting Indigenous communities and efforts to intergenerationally transmit cultural knowledge through artistic traditions and interventions.

Divided into four parts, the main themes simultaneously represent a set of priorities that Indigenous artists, alongside coeditors Bunn-Marcuse and Jonaitis, have identified as central to future research and interventions into Northwest Coast art studies. Each essay speaks to the core of what it means to "unsettle Native art history" by reframing how Indigenous art is valued, understood, and appreciated by both Indigenous and non-Indigenous people (4). Throughout the volume, the ideological veil of Western categorization is removed and reconsidered in the context of Indigenous authority and knowledge. Additionally, the authors reflect upon and enact current ethical standards that acknowledge the rights, authority, and expertise of Indigenous Peoples over their histories and artistic traditions. Both Indigenous and non-Indigenous experts lead the way in the development of new Northwest Coast art studies scholarship by "weaving knowledge through the warps of settler colonialism" and identifying Indigenous priorities including the embodiment of survivance, kinship, connection to land, and sovereignty (14).

The editors and contributors bring Indigenous voices to the forefront by providing a deeper understanding of how Indigenous Peoples experience their art beyond aesthetic value and by reframing art as cultural patrimony part of a larger network of knowledge. This volume weaves historical narratives shaped by Western thought together with Indigenous knowledge, central to the theme of recognizing Indigenous rights and authority over their traditions. As the title suggests, Native people have been and continue to be involved in shaping the very fields and markets in which their work circulates. Christopher Green states in his chapter on Tlingit artist Jim Schoppert's artistic philosophies, "Indigenous art is compatible with innovation" (57) and remains a visioning board for Indigenous sovereignty and survivance where art is the transmission of cultural histories (118).

Within this volume, Indigenous artistic histories are reflected on through an Indigenous concept (originating from the Cherokee language) of the "longer now," which Bunn-Marcuse defines as "understanding how our current moment is part of the longer history that surrounds us, connecting past to present to future with awareness of our responsibilities across these generations" (4). Lou-Ann Ika'wega Neel builds upon the concept of a "longer now" by sharing a journey of reconnection to her grandmother's legacy while developing her own artistic style against the colonial pressures over who can practice traditions such as totem carving (133). Reconnection for Indigenous artists, like Neel, is largely made possible by institutions such as libraries, archives, and museums, many of which are in the process of collaboratively reconciling with historical wrongdoings and developing standards of care and documentation of Indigenous materials. Aldona Jonaitis and Janet Catherine Berlo state it is critical to analyze stories, actions, and objects "in light of their particular and varying historical trajectories and imperatives" in relation to Indigenous art and institutions (89). As Bunn-Marcuse states, the act of unsettling "requires work that is actively aware of both past and ongoing effects of settler colonialism; commits listening, learning, and acting in ways that respect and uphold Indigenous priorities; and calls for or demonstrates new practices based in this awareness and accountability to the impacts of scholarly work" (4).

*Unsettling* offers scholars, students, and communities a timely and critical gathering of intergenerational knowledge that brings the Native point of view to the forefront of a field that has historically assumed authority over the narratives of Indigenous artistic traditions. The collaborative nature of this volume accentuates the need for scholars, curators, and institutions in general to engage in reciprocal dialogue with both Indigenous communities and the past, present, and future of our "longer now" and the histories that have shaped our understanding of Native art on the Northwest Coast.

**BRANDON CASTLE** is a member of the Tsimshian Nation and Ketchikan Indian Community. He is currently the project coordinator for Mapping Native Intellectual Networks of the Northeast at Amherst College in Amherst, Massachusetts.

# MARGARET JACOBS

*Taking Children: A History of American Terror*
by Laura Briggs
University of California Press, 2020

MANY AMERICANS LOOKED ON in horror as the Trump administration ordered the Department of Homeland Security to separate more than two thousand migrant and refugee children from their families at the U.S.-Mexico border in 2018. Laura Briggs argues that there is an important historical context for this child-taking that is often missing from public debates. By recovering this history, Briggs contends that we can respond more effectively to the human rights abuses of child separation in our own time.

In just 178 pages, Briggs outlines the long history of separating children from their families in North America. She points out that this has been a "strategy for terrorizing people for centuries" (7). Slaveowners routinely sold children away from their kin. U.S. support for right-wing Latin American dictatorships in the late twentieth century turned a blind eye to their common practice of taking children from left-wing families. The war on drugs disproportionately affected parents of color; the mass incarceration it triggered served as a child separation program. As Briggs explains, "The criminalization of families of color, and the widespread taking of their children in to foster care for petty or imagined crimes, provided the template for taking children at the border" (127).

Briggs also devotes a chapter to discussing how Native Americans endured more than a century of child removal through the U.S. government's Indian boarding school policy and the promotion of fostering and adoption in non-Indian families after World War II.

Briggs attributes all of these disparate instances of taking children to "a counterinsurgency tactic [that] has been used to respond to demands for rights, refuge, and respect by communities of color and impoverished communities" (12–13). This seems a particularly trenchant observation in relation to the cases Briggs covers in Central America. Right-wing governments in El Salvador and Guatemala were kidnapping the children of activists they claimed were Communist insurgents. There is also evidence that authorities, whether slave owners or government officials, used child removal to undermine resistance of enslaved people and American Indian families and force them to comply.

For example, Briggs points out that AIM activist Leonard Peltier was convicted based on the testimony of Myrtle Poor Bear, who later recanted her testimony. She revealed that the FBI had threatened to take her daughter and told her she would never see her child again if Poor Bear did not cooperate with the FBI and sign a statement declaring that she had seen Peltier shoot FBI agents.

Briggs's background as a historian of both Latin America and of adoption enables her to make important connections between U.S. foreign and domestic policy. Her previous book, *Somebody's Children: The Politics of Transracial and Transnational Adoption*, compares how adoption practices in the U.S. have represented assaults on African American and Native American communities as well as impoverished Central American families.

Briggs's counter-insurgency explanation for stealing children provides a valuable theme that runs throughout the book. The book might have given more attention to the way in which child removal served as a protean strategy that had other purposes, depending on the group that was targeted. Briggs mentions some of these other purposes. She notes that in Guatemala, "The goal of disappearing children came from the logic of ideological *and* genocidal elimination." Many families whom the Guatemalan government targeted were of Indigenous descent, and child removal "disrupt[ed] the transmission of languages, ways of life, the practical arts of weaving *huipiles* (blouses), ways of thinking and acting" (92).

Briggs's book could benefit from drawing this analysis out further and covering in more depth how authorities separated Indigenous children from their families to support settler-colonialism goals of eliminating Indigenous Peoples and stealing their land as much, or even more perhaps, than counter-insurgency.

Still, *Taking Children* serves as a powerful manifesto that makes important connections between disparate policies and practices. Briggs also shows that there is a "fierce tradition of protesting this practice" (13), including how Native nations fought for the Indian Child Welfare Act to reclaim the care of their children. The book may help to promote greater solidarity and activism among many different groups that have been so unjustly targeted for child removal.

**MARGARET JACOBS** is a professor in the Department of History and Center for Great Plains Studies, University of Nebraska-Lincoln.

# KEITLYN ALCANTARA

*Native Foodways: Indigenous North American Religious Traditions and Foods*
edited by Michelene E. Pensatubbee and Michael J. Zogry
SUNY Press, 2021

WRITTEN AT THE INTERSECTION of poetry, gratitude practice, and historical case study, *Native Foodways: Indigenous North American Religious Traditions and Foods* recontextualizes foodways research by weaving it inextricably with spirituality. Across an edited volume of eight chapters, an introduction, and epilogue, the authors navigate foodways as interconnected relationships that balance the needs and responsibilities of all living beings on the landscape. Traditional Ecological Knowledge is seen as all encompassing, with stories, dances, rituals, and ethics of cross-species respect forming parts of the same ecological whole that is the key to resilience. Daily practices of engagement become the science, teaching skills of humility, deep listening, and wonder. Together, the essays in this collection exist across time, providing historical context, critique of the present, and concrete visions of a future of reclaiming, relearning, and recentering Indigenous relationships with land.

The essays bring embodiment into the sensorially flattened world of the written word in content as well as in form. Lawrence W. Gross's chapter 4, "Harvesting Wild Rice," is a veritable gift to the reader, drawing together imagery, sound, and movement to imbue the pages with the embodied experience of *manoomin* harvest. Suzanne Crawford O'Brien's chapter 2, "Of Coyotes and Culverts: Salmon and the People of the Mid-Columbia River," maps creation stories onto the landscape as "stories that teach ethical ways of living alongside the plant and animal people" (55). The collection is academically innovative yet rooted in traditional forms of knowing and teaching. Each chapter successfully contributes to the "commitment to treat as authentic the cultural products of Indigenous communities, and to accord them the same veracity as archaeological evidence and written evidence arranged in a linear chronology" (6–7) laid out within Michael J. Zogry's introduction.

A repeated lesson throughout is the decentering of humans as the primary actors in the natural world, placing emphasis on plant and animal beings as active agents capable of rescinding collective participation if their own needs are not being met or respected. In chapter 5, "They Call us 'Caribou Eaters': Negotiating Tłįchǫ Dene Relationships with Caribou," David S. Walsh explores how, in Tłįchǫ territories, the decline in the Caribou population is not just due to overhunting or pollution of the landscape but to a mindful distancing by Caribou intent on protecting their own emotional and spiritual life. In chapter 3, "Where Food Grows on the Water: *Manoomin/* Wild Rice and Anishinaabe Peoplehood," Michael D. McNally discusses *manoominikewin* (harvesting wild rice) as both a verb and a rule of engagement that considers *manoomin*'s right to life as an inhabitant of the landscape. Crawford O'Brien and Woghan discuss similar themes in chapter 6 in relation to Tepary beans, salmon, huckleberries, and Yaupon holly, with these beings honored as "not merely resources, but relatives and ancestors" (142). In terms of ecological sustainability, the goal is not to place humans as protectors and stewards but rather as interlocutors who have much to learn from the wisdom of the vast landscape community.

By incorporating place-based histories of colonialism, the authors show the diverse yet analogous patterns of displacement and forced rupture of cross-species community in Indigenous North America. Creating space for the grief of this immense loss, the authors simultaneously center future-facing projects aimed at reviving these practices and rebuilding relationships with plant and animal beings (e.g., Tohono O'odham Community Action; Tłįchǫ Traditional Caribou Conservation; Keeping Our Community Healthy; the Nisqually Community Garden). In chapter 6, "Bringing a Berry Back from the Land of the Dead: Coast Salish Huckleberry Cultivation and Food Sovereignty," Suzanne Crawford O'Brien and Kimberly Wogahn pointedly call out Euro-American-driven alternative and "local" food movements for their acute avoidance of reckoning with the accumulated and ongoing violence of settler colonialism. To simply "return to the land" without acknowledging this history of colonization and forced removal is to force society woundedly forward without conscience for continued pain inflicted on Native communities. By contrast, Native-driven movements draw on foodways to map this history into the present. Such is the example in chapter 8, "The Semiotics of Resistance: On the Power of Frybread" by Dennis Kelley, which illustrates how, even with hybrid offerings like frybread, food continues to serve as a link between "social, spiritual, cultural, and natural systems,"[1] embodying life beyond colonialism.

The applications of these chapters span endless possibilities within scholarly thought. Yet their power is also in their adherence to the realm of *being*, of ideas lived through practice. In the epilogue, Michelene E. Pesantubbee reflects on eating as "ceremony welcoming and thanking the other-than-human people for making themselves available to humans" (211). Similarly, the authors of these collective essays offer up the possibility of foodways studies as research, ceremony, and ritual.

**KEITLYN ALCANTARA** is assistant professor of anthropology at Indiana University, Bloomington.

## Note

1. See chap. 2, p. 64 of *Native Foodways*; original quote is from the Columbia River Intertribal Fish Commission website, https://critfc.org/.

# JESSICA BISSETT PEREA

*Staging Indigeneity: Salvage Tourism and the Performance*
*of Native American History*
by Katrina M. Phillips
University of North Carolina Press, 2021

**IT WOULD BE EASY** for NAIS scholars to dismiss staged Native-inspired histori-cal dramas, or "Indian Pageants," created for tourist audiences as cheesy or unimportant; as yet more projects in a long line of projects designed by and for settler audiences to further cement settler futurities. Yet Katrina M. Phillips's excellent new book *Staging Indigeneity: Salvage Tourism and the Performance of Native American History* persuasively argues that such prob-lematic performances require our attention.

By constructing acts Phillips calls "salvage tourism," Indian pageants "use American Indian history to help rescue regional economies" (7) via pro-cesses and practices "created by and performed for non-Natives" (12) that eschew historical accuracy by instead privileging the "spirit of history" (20). While related to familiar forms of salvage ethnography and heritage tour-ism, Phillips argues that salvage tourism is distinct in its orientation toward saving settler economies, bolstering settler histories, and thus strengthen-ing settler senses of self (12). For some rural communities with fragile econ-omies, destination tourism functions as one of the last exploitable natural resources and relies on emphasizing how specific places uniquely augment a production's authenticity as "dramatic reenactments 'in the exact spots' where the exciting action had originally occurred" (5). Phillips details how staged Indian pageants assert and confer attributes of Indigeneity—attri-butes that are divorced from actual Indigenous Peoples—to commodified versions of Native Peoples, places, and (hi)stories in ways that also invite non-Native tourists to make pilgrimages to so-called "holy grounds" (19) to partake in salvation via acts of "historical communion" (8). Indeed, Phil-lips's provocative invocations of religiosity through terms such as "salva-tion," "pilgrimage," "communion," and "spirit" recall the fervor with which the Protestant U.S. nation-state came into being and further articulate the critical need to understand the role performing arts play in nation-building projects. *Staging Indigeneity* explains how performances of Native Ameri-can history "produced by, packaged for, and consumed by non-Natives" (10) are inextricably intertwined with a maintenance of colonial narratives and structures.

Phillips's work weaves together a rigorous cross-continental archival and ethnographic research program "from the dusty ranges of Oregon to the mountains of North Carolina to the pastoral feel of southern Ohio" (185). Her book offers three case studies, each centered on the development of one twentieth-century outdoor drama, to address the ways in which tourist productions steeped in settler romanticism, nostalgia, and sentimentalism relate to broader issues about Indian identity, authenticity, citizenship, and belonging. Phillips's treatment of the three pageants, presented in order of premiere date, places them in conversation with histories and economies of each area's Indigenous Peoples, including: (1) "Happy Canyon Indian Pageant and Wild West Show" in Pendleton, Oregon (ca. 1916) and the Confederated Tribes of the Umatilla Indian Reservation; (2) *Unto These Hills* in Cherokee, North Carolina (ca. 1950s), and the Eastern Band of Cherokee Indians; and (3) *Tecumseh!* in Chillicothe, Ohio (ca. 1973), and Shawnee Peoples (Absentee Shawnee Tribe, the Shawnee Tribe, and the Eastern Shawnee Tribe of Oklahoma). Each of the three case studies features a pair of chapters: the first offers historical context and insight into the production's origins; the second discusses Native Peoples' presence within and relationships to each production in general, while also highlighting Native Peoples' cultural and economic interests more specifically. Notably, Phillips takes a care-filled approach when discussing Native participation in these stagings. While the Confederated Tribes of the Umatilla Indian Reservation and the Eastern Band of Cherokee Indians found ways to assert agency and advance some aspects of their community's health and well-being, Shawnee Peoples remain a present and misrepresented absence within re-created and reinvented settler histories about Tecumseh's "failure" (179), which continue to disappear them with each subsequent performance. Taken together, Phillips deftly addresses multiple stakes and stakeholders of salvage tourism.

In conclusion, and returning to the book's title, Phillips joins a growing cohort of Native American and Indigenous performance studies scholars who argue for explanations of Indigeneity as more than simply the condition of *being* Indigenous; Indigeneity must instead account for the inextricably intertwined ways of *knowing* (analytics or logics) and *doing* (practices or projects) that inform performances or understandings of identity (ways of being). Phillips's book contributes further insights into the densities of Indigeneity through in-depth examinations of non-Native projects that stage Native Peoples and places, which remind us how the term "Indigeneity" is always already tethered to notions of coloniality, a fact marked by its

English language formulations. *Staging Indigeneity* provides NAIS readers with new frameworks for approaching seemingly marginal or commodified productions in ways that uplift Indigenous-led resurgence and futurities.

JESSICA BISSETT PEREA (Dena'ina) is an interdisciplinary musician-scholar and associate professor of Native American Studies at the University of California, Davis.

# CAROLINE FIDAN TYLER DOENMEZ

*Collective Care: Indigenous Motherhood, Family, and HIV/AIDS*
by Pamela J. Downe
University of Toronto Press, 2021

**DESPITE THE ROBUST BODY OF RESEARCH** addressing various dimensions of HIV/AIDS, very little has been written about the families impacted by this epidemic. Pamela Downe's *Collective Care* endeavors to fill this gap and counter the presumption that motherhood and HIV/AIDS are "irreconcilable categories" (34). The ethnography is animated by the question: "What does it mean to be a mother in the context of HIV/AIDS?" (3) Downe responds to this inquiry in five substantive chapters that draw on narrative-style interviews and participant observation research, emerging out of a collaborative project that she undertook with People Who Access Services (PWAS) at an organization called AIDS Saskatoon. A unique methodological dimension of the text is a "photovoice" project, in which participants took pictures to reflect "what it means to be a parent in the context of HIV/AIDS in Saskatchewan" (15). In the opening section, Downe thoughtfully accounts for her positionality as a non-Indigenous anthropologist, addressing her commitments to Indigenous rights and decolonizing research. Throughout the book, she foregrounds the voices and stories of her Indigenous participants to develop her central claim that collective care is a vital form of mothering for women living with HIV/AIDS and a "cultural touchstone" that sustains community bonds and ensures the well-being of children (viii). The author shows how this form of kinship challenges widely accepted Euro-North American concepts of family roles, exceeding biological definitions of parenthood and involving a wide array of figures who assume caregiving responsibilities for one another. She highlights how collective care is often misperceived as negligent, irresponsible, and unmotherly by the public and various institutional figures, including teachers, police, and social workers. Against this stigma, collective care endures as an invaluable source of support and belonging for families living with HIV/AIDS.

Saskatchewan has the highest rates of HIV/AIDS of any province in Canada and Indigenous people—specifically women of child-bearing age—are vastly overrepresented in these numbers. Downe is emphatic that the epidemic is a product of state-sanctioned and structural violence, asserting: "In Saskatchewan, the forced disruption and dislocation of Indigenous societies underpins the HIV virus, disease and death" (14). She engages syndemic theory to argue that HIV/AIDS is not a stand-alone issue but rather intimately interrelated with other health conditions, including the hepatitis C virus, injection drug use, and opioid addiction, all of which are driven by the legacies and ongoing impacts of settler colonial dispossession and intergenerational trauma.

One of these persistent forms of colonial violence that Downe examines is the devastating trend of Indigenous child removal by social workers. Her chapters chronicle how parents and caregivers live with the pervasive threat of losing their children and how they are constantly subjected to the expectation of parental failure by virtue of their addictions or diagnoses. Through the stories of her participants, she provides critical documentation of these women's experiences of having their children removed, illustrating the punitive, exhausting, and deleterious effects of this system of child welfare. As one participant stated: "All of us Aboriginal moms, all of us HIV moms, we live with this nightmare all the time" (25). Her interlocutors' narratives reveal how their perceived shortcomings as parents often result from their involvement in collective care-giving networks that are misinterpreted as "neglectful" by authorities. Moreover, Downe argues that there is "a colonizing nature to the politics of individualistic motherhood" (54) in that those who are regarded as deviating from this norm are subjected to increased scrutiny and judgment. She deftly demonstrates that this damaging stigma does not correspond to the reality of her participants' dedication to raising, protecting, and nurturing their children.

*Collective Care* unsettles dominant assumptions about motherhood, family, and care, detailing how these culturally specific understandings are socially and historically situated. This provocation prompts readers to interrogate deeply ingrained notions of what constitutes worthy parenthood and a desirable family unit. The book invites further scholarly attention to the ways in which contemporary Indigenous family life is targeted by settler colonial forms of surveillance and control, and how Indigenous caregiving practices contest and transcend these logics. By centering the participants' lived experiences and theories, this ethnography vividly and compellingly illustrates how HIV/AIDS impacts entire family networks, and how meaningful responses to the epidemic must address it on this collective level. This rigorous, accessible text will be a valuable resource for scholars in Native American and Indigenous studies and sociocultural and medical anthropology, and it should be required reading for students of medicine, criminal justice, and social work.

CAROLINE FIDAN TYLER DOENMEZ is a doctoral candidate in the Department of Anthropology at the University of Minnesota and a visiting scholar in the Department of Native American and Indigenous Studies at Dartmouth College.

# COLTON BRANDAU

*Space-Time Colonialism: Alaska's Indigenous and Asian*
*   Entanglements*
by Juliana Hu Pegues
University of North Carolina Press, 2021

JULIANA HU PEGUES'S *Space-Time Colonialism: Alaska's Indigenous and Asian Entanglements* challenges established assumptions about Native and Asian immigrant peoples in what is now known as Alaska through a discussion of the former's temporal and the latter's spatial exclusions. Building upon theoretical frameworks from Jodi Byrd, Lisa Lowe, and Iyko Day, Hu Pegues employs the term "space-time colonialism" to both draw attention to the "generative potential" of a relational and intimate framework in discussing temporal and spatial analyses of colonialism and to "consider the messy and overlapping spaces and times of imperial conquest and colonial governance" (13—14). Examining an extensive range of materials, from government documents to newspapers to Asian American and Alaska Native literatures, Hu Pegues argues that Native and Asian relational possibilities demonstrate how "imperial and settler colonial statecraft" both operates and conceals itself in Alaska (18).

In her first case study, Hu Pegues critiques settler travel documents and ethnographies created after the U.S. (so-called) Purchase of Alaska, which envisions the territory's Native Peoples as "Asiatic." This configuration of settler orientalism and its "racialized intimacy" supported overlapping notions of Alaska as an imperial/settler colonial space and emphasized Alaska Natives as "distinct and exceptional" (21—22). Subsequently, this distinction validated the supposed foreignness of Alaska Natives and disregarded the presence of regional Asian laborers. Her second chapter analyzes narratives of the Gold Rush and the figure named China Joe in Southeastern Alaskan history. Contrasting his story of providing for white townspeople with narratives of Chinese expulsions in 1886 and hangings of Tlingit persons three years earlier, Hu Pegues emphasizes the role of settler masculinity and terroristic violence in establishing dominance over Asian and Native bodies and lands; the former were excluded due to their perceived "spatial excess," while the latter, through "unpredictable and prolonged" colonial formations, found themselves temporally removed (78).

In her third chapter, Hu Pegues deconstructs scholarship on Asian/Native labor in salmon canneries, arguing a focus on "productivity" constructs an image that does not account for Asian and Native intimacies across race, gender, and sexuality. Examining literary works by Nora Dauenhauer (Tlingit) and Carlos Bulosan (Filipino), she challenges this productivity framework, asserting that both authors articulate notions of intimacy within cannery experiences that contest "an emergent industrialism and a heteronormative nation-state" (116). For her last case study, Hu Pegues examines photographic works by Shoki Kayamori, a Japanese immigrant who for several decades lived in Yakutat among Tlingit and non-Native Peoples. Investigating his images of Native boarding school students, individual/group portraits, and local chapters of the Alaska Native Brotherhood, Hu Pegues argues Kayamori's photographic representations depict "a powerful articulation of intimacy from the failed settler subject position of alien resident" (121). His story also fosters examinations of World War II militarism through Japanese and Unangax̂ internments in Alaska to "account for the colonial violence inherent in settler modernity and prioritize decolonial strategies within transpacific critique" (152).

As a discursive and regional work, the book succeeds exceptionally. It offers an important contribution to the discipline of Alaska Native studies, which has often been dominated by older anthropological discourses. Additionally, Hu Pegues proposes a generative relationship between NAIS and Asian American Studies beyond a settler-immigrant-Indigenous formation through examining Alaskan histories neglected by similar works on racialization and settler colonialism. Her regional focus is also significant, although particular. Given the wealth of resources written by, for, and with Tlingit Peoples and Hu Pegues's multiple connections to Lingit Aani [Tlingit homelands in Southeastern Alaska], her primary focus on histories, experiences, and literatures in this region is practical. However, while seemingly limited, the concentration on these spaces and Native Nations is not necessarily a hindrance but an invitation for future research.

Over the last few decades, Native American and Indigenous studies has involved more prominent discussions of Alaska Native literary and theoretical works. Further, in 2020, legal challenges to Alaska Native Corporations (ANCs) receiving COVID relief monies based upon their perceived distinctiveness from Native American Nations reignited discourses of Alaska Native exceptionalism. *Space-Time Colonialism* is a welcome and exciting contribution to these historic ongoing conversations. While focusing on Alaska, Hu Pegues also offers important insights into other settler/Indigenous discourses. Juxtaposing this book with works such as Maile Arvin's *Possessing Polynesians* and Maria Saldaña-Portillo's *Indian Given* offers insightful understandings of interplays between race, colonialism, and Indigeneity in imperial, visual, and historical contexts. Not only scholars of Alaska Native studies specifically but of Asian American and Native American and Indigenous studies in general will benefit from engaging with this work and the future scholarship it influences.

**COLTON BRANDAU** is a Ph.D. candidate in Native American studies at the University of California, Davis

# LAURA BRIGGS

*Intimate Integration: A History of the Sixties Scoop
and the Colonization of Indigenous Kinship*
by Allyson D. Stevenson
University of Toronto Press, 2021

**INTIMATE INTEGRATION** is an ambitious book that sets out not just to tell us about Canada's "Sixties Scoop" of Native children into foster care but also what kinship means for policymakers, Métis, and Indigenous People. It centers on Saskatchewan, a narrow enough focus that we can see the effects of both provincial and federal policy. Saskatchewan is also where Stevenson was born and raised as a Métis adoptee before getting her Ph.D. and becoming a professional scholar.

Since the earliest days of the settlement of the interior of Canada by the Hudson Bay Company and those who traded with Cree, Assiniboine, and Dene for furs, there has been a significant Métis population produced through intermarriage and more casual and even violent relationships. However, when Canada reached a settlement agreement with Status Indian and Inuit people over what is often called the "Sixties Scoop," the massive apprehension of children on reserves into care under the slightest pretext— in what social workers themselves admit was an effort to "save" children from Native poverty by taking them—the federal government did not include Métis children because they were taken under the jurisdiction of provincial (not federal) agents. Further, though the reckoning with residential schools in Canada went through a Truth and Reconciliation Commission process, the settlement agreement with Métis children (and the adults they became) who spent time in foster care and adoptions never offered those who lost kin and cultural connection the opportunity to tell their stories. Hence this book, which among its many contributions includes oral histories of Métis adoptees.

Stevenson examines many kinds of disruption of family ties, including the assimilationist Canadian policy of passing Indian status only through the male line, so women who married non-Indigenous People and children fathered by someone who is not Native cannot claim Indian status and had to leave their home communities. Status policy wreaked havoc with kin relationships, disrupting the care of grandparents, aunts, and uncles, even when children were not taken into residential schools or foster care. As a further consequence, Canada developed large Métis populations around reserves and on unused Crown land. Because these communities did not own their land, they did not pay taxes and thus were not permitted to send their children to school. As a result, Métis people were painted as shiftless, failed farmers with men refusing to act as breadwinners and women failing to be effective housewives (in unheated shacks) or mothers (because children denied schooling were less conventionally "successful."). These outcomes, in turn, justified taking children into care.

We do not encounter the kind of story that most expect from a book like this until the sixth chapter, which focuses on the mid-twentieth-century Adopt Indian and Métis (AIM) Program and the Adoption Resource Exchange of North America (ARENA). There are good reasons to not make this the narrative center of the book. While the spectacle of U.S. and Canadian governments deliberately moving children from Native and Métis families to white ones seems to capture the Indigenous genocide from which white families benefit and that lies at the heart of North American settler colonialism, these were actually quite small programs. Stevenson says that 3.5 to 4.5 percent of Indian and Métis children who were apprehended into foster care were placed in adoptive families. Adoption is not the main story, which is really about the federal government and provinces taking children into care (also true in the U.S.).

I am glad to see this book pull the lens back from the adoption question and hope it is a harbinger for the field. As we think in ever-greater numbers about the consequences of reliance on policing to solve social problems, we need more histories of the causes and consequences of family policing through taking children for reasons of so-called neglect that in fact are the result of poverty.

While many scholars have explored the centrality of imposing Euro-North American gender and kinship systems to settler colonialism's land grabs, Stevenson does far more explicit work in linking it to the taking of children into foster care. "The colonization of kinship violently sundered not only intimate and familial ties but also the geopolitical connection that extend beyond human relations to encompass ties to land, animals, and ancestors that make up Indigenous identity," she writes (41). Stevenson makes a significant contribution, and we are richer for it.

LAURA BRIGGS is professor of women, gender, and sexuality studies at the University of Massachusetts.

# PAUL McKENZIE-JONES

*Chief Thunderwater: An Unexpected Indian in Unexpected Places*
by Gerald F. Reid
University of Oklahoma Press, 2021

**REID HAS PRODUCED** an exceptionally well-researched biography of a somewhat controversial but also largely ignored Indigenous advocate for tribal self-determination in early twentieth-century United States and Canada. The provocative introduction retells the commonly understood narrative of Chief Thunderwater as an impostor, fraud, and conman—a reputation Reid dissects throughout the book—and his political movement as the vehicle for that fraud. The fact that this retelling is from an academic article published in 1965 in a reputable journal immediately leads the reader to ask: Who was this man? How is Reid going to tell his story?

In answer to the first question, according to Reid's research and the documents/testimony he examined, Oghema Niagara, or Chief Thunderwater as he was more commonly known, was a complicated, larger-than-life, Indigenous activist and a critical component of Haudenosaunee political revitalization in the early 1900s. The answer to the second question is that Reid tells his story compellingly, including exposing the smear campaigns that resulted in Thunderwater being essentially written out of history as a fake for almost a century. The campaigns were largely orchestrated by members of the Society of American Indians (SAI) and later by Duncan Campbell Scott, in his role as Canada's deputy superintendent general of Indian affairs, highlighting how key a figure Thunderwater was in the sovereignty movement of the early 1900s.

Reid traces the beginning of Thunderwater's activism to Cleveland, Ohio, where he pushed back against U.S. federal assimilationist policies and especially local women's church organizations championing those policies. His early activism led to the creation of the Council of the Tribes, a movement/organization modeled on the Haudenosaunee political organization of the Six Nations Confederacy, a model that quickly drew Thunderbird's attention to Haudenosaunee rights to freely cross the U.S./Canadian border and their continuous attempts to protect those rights, several years before the more celebrated border activism of Tuscarora Chief Clinton Rickard and his Indian Defense League of America.

Reid argues that Thunderwater's involvement in the border rights issues led to his deeper involvement in Haudenosaunee political revitalization on the Canadian side of the international border. His first Council of the Indians meeting in Canada was held at Kahnewake, and the movement subsequently spread across other communities and reserves, ultimately leading to a growth of Council of the Tribes chapters. As the council grew, multiple members of his movement began to get elected to leadership positions across various band councils. The growth and popularity of his movement and its political ideas led Arthur Parker of the SAI to contact Duncan Campbell Scott with accusations of Thunderwater's racial fraud. Scott was a willing audience to Parker's accusations and almost immediately used them as the springboard to launch a smear campaign to discredit Thunderwater and weaken his influence across Haudenosaunee politics.

Reid shows how the Canadian government's smear campaign was successful, leading to newspaper coverage "exposing" Thunderwater and a subsequent libel case that went unresolved. While not exclusively the reason for Thunderwater's waning influence on Haudenosaunee politics—the rise of other leaders and movements, such as Laura Cornelius Kellogg's great influence after she left the SAI, and F. O. Loft's creation of the League of Indians of Canada were also factors—it was certainly a determining factor, especially in how his reputation remained tarnished long after his death.

The news coverage and libel suit exemplify the larger controversies that marked Thunderwater's life; Reid covers these areas with the same attention to detail as he gives Thunderwater's activism. Ultimately, this text reintroduces a too-long-silenced figure in the long history of the Indigenous fight for self-determination in the United States and Canada. Long derided as a fraud and consigned to the fringes of history as a result, Thunderwater's reputation is now at least partially restored—personal controversies notwithstanding—as a result of Reid's fair, compelling, and exceptionally well-researched biography.

**PAUL McKENZIE-JONES** is associate professor of Indigenous studies at the University of Lethbridge, Alberta.

# CRYSTAL GAIL FRASER

*Our Whole Gwich'in Way of Life Has Changed / Gwich'in K'yuu*
   *Gwiidandài' Tthak Ejuk Gòonlih Stories from the People of the Land*
by Leslie McCartney and The Gwich'in Tribal Council
University of Alberta Press, 2020

THIS MAGNIFICENT, 848-PAGE VOLUME by anthropologist Leslie McCartney and the Gwich'in Tribal Council (GTC) includes the oral histories of Dinjii Zhuh Elders: the lived experiences of eighteen women and six men. The book is "structured to give the reader a general background to the Gwich'in people and their traditional lands" (xvi). Histories of northern Canada and Indigenous Peoples who have inhabited those Lands since Time Immemorial are few and far between; this collection makes a significant contribution to our understanding of Dinjii Zhuh histories, the methodology of oral histories, and Indigenous engagement in scholarly research.

As reflected during my lifetime as a Gwichyà Gwich'in woman, the dominant voices in this collection of personal narratives are Elders. Again and again, they command our attention and demonstrate their expertise in their use of our language (Dinjii Zhuh Ginjik) and on-the-Land skills such as hunting, moosehide tanning, traveling, and parenting. With all Indigenous testimonies, the hard histories of colonialism, Indian Residential Schooling, disease, and trauma lie just below the surface, but they are countered by the radiant sense of humor among Dinjii Zhuh. Elder Sarah Ann (Firth) Gardlund says, "Lots of times, funny things happened to me" as she recounts her delight in winning curling matches against the aggrieved white schoolteacher in Aklavik (260).

When our own people undertake research related to Dinjii Zhuh, it warms my heart. I can turn to very few books that document the words of my maternal grandmother, delicate information about her mother, and the history of our people—Dinjii Zhuh—more generally. This collection represents how one generation understood not only our identities but also our responsibilities. My grandmother Marka (née Andre) Bullock recorded her story for this volume when she was seventy-five years old. I often visited her during this time, and Marka had already begun thinking about her transition to the next world, which was grounded in the importance of our fish camp and the seasonal nature of our culture and lifestyle: "Sometimes I think if

I get lost, if I just go to Tsiigehtshik and lose myself, and continue my journey to Dachan Choo Géhnjik, that's where they will find me. I would be just happy. I would go very happy" (569). Because of Marka, I continue to return to Dachan Choo Géhnjik where I learn the lessons of how to be a matriarch on our Land, at our fish camp, and alongside my young daughter. The crucial role that Dinjii Zhuh women played and their connection to the Land not only runs through Marka's story but among all twenty-four life narratives, whether told by women or men.

Dinjii Zhuh Elders frequently state, "Listen to what I'm saying," which is the title of chapter 25. Here, McCartney and the GTC seek to bridge the divide between the people of a generation who grew up on the Land with Dinjii Zhuh values and the younger generation living in the Dinjii Zhuh diaspora who may not be connected to their families, Homelands, and ancestral teachings. These "Gwich'in values include respect, honour, love, kindness, dance/song, laughter/humour, teaching, our stories, spirituality, honesty and fairness, sharing, and caring. In their stories, the Elders spoke of all of these things" (621–22). Because these values were documented and now available to all Dinjii Zhuh, we can collectively learn new ways to make and sustain relationships, care for our children and families, and go forward with our lives in a good and ancestral way.

As a testament to the intent of this book—a resource for Dinjii Zhuh citizens and community—related scholarly literature is not discussed until the concluding chapter where the book "can be nested within the existing anthropological and oral history literature" (xviii). Placing a literature review at the back of the book not only accommodates the audience but also speaks to the community-engaged nature of this collection. For Indigenous Peoples, relationships with academia have a complex and sometimes vexed history, but the scholarship used and modeled in *Gwich'in K'yuu Gwiidandài' Tthak Ejuk Gòonlih* charts an innovative, ethical, and respectful path for Indigenous research.

This book is essential reading for Dinjii Zhuh citizens, students, academics, and anyone else who is interested in Dinjii Zhuh history and Indigenous research methodologies. In this timeless piece, McCartney and the GTC have centered and elevated the words of our Elders in a way that remains unmatched in today's scholarship on northern Canada.

CRYSTAL GAIL FRASER, Gwichyà Gwich'in historian from Inuvik and Dachan Choo Géhnjik in the Northwest Territories, Canada, is assistant professor in the Department of History, Classics, and Religion and the Faculty of Native Studies at the University of Alberta.

# JEFFREY D. BURNETTE

*Indigenous Data Sovereignty and Policy*
edited by Maggie Walter, Tahu Kukutai, Stephanie Russo Carroll,
    and Desi Rodriguez-Lonebear
Taylor & Francis, 2021

STATISTICS HAVE LONG BEEN USED as a tool for shaping the narrative about Indigenous People, communities, and nations through the use of 5 D data—"a set of items related almost exclusively to measure Indigenous difference, disparity, disadvantage, dysfunction and deprivation" (9). This pathologizing approach to data creation and analysis has led to dysfunctional policies that are then used to justify the need for more data focused on the 5 Ds and that shape dominant society's understanding of Indigenous People.

*Indigenous Data Sovereignty and Policy* drives home the problematic nature of this approach to data collection and analysis through the use of case studies while centering the discussion on Indigenous data sovereignty (IDS) and Indigenous data governance (IGOV). The editors have assembled a wide array of examples that demonstrate the many ways that data has developed dominant society's incomplete and inaccurate understanding of Indigenous People, communities, and nations. At the same time, the anthology enables readers to connect common themes that are consistently applied to national datasets across countries.

Chapter 1 by Walter and Carroll establishes the strong foundation between IDS, IGOV, and government policy that makes the edited volume's approach work by defining IDS and discussing how colonial states use data to construct narratives of difference. Walter and Carroll detail how IDS and IGOV combat current dominant narratives and describes current national IDS networks. Chapter 15 by Walter, Carroll, Kukutai, and Rodriguez-Lonebear usefully closes the topic by reflecting on the challenges and opportunities facing the IDS movement and summarizing earlier chapters.

Each chapter in between these bookends provides a case study that exemplifies either: (1) IDS in a specific area; (2) how data is used to create contested narratives; or (3) how Indigenous nations are succeeding in creating and governing their own data. For example, chapters 2, 3, 5, and 6 describe and analyze IDS in Aotearoa New Zealand, Australia, and Canada, while other chapters extend the analysis to include Colombia, Mexico, Spain, Sweden, and the United States. Chapters 4 and 10 detail successful examples of Pueblo and Quechan data sovereignty in practice. More importantly, they also demonstrate the key role that values and culture play in shaping what data is created, discussing their process and describing lessons learned. In chapter 7, Bengoetxea examines how the lack of agency and fear concerning the misuse of ethnicity data has rendered Sami People invisible in national population statistics. Chapters 11, 13, and 14 connect IDS to other areas or disciplines. The ways universities and Institutional Review Boards can support IDS are presented in chapter 11, while chapter 14 focuses on its legal dimensions. Chapter 13 by Paine, Cormack, Reid, Harris, and Robson demonstrates how the choice of statistical technique and framing privilege non-Indigenous communities. For instance, certain statistics like morbidity rates are standardized to allow comparisons across different groups. For morbidity rates, the age structure of non-Indigenous populations is used for standardization, ensuring morbidity rates more accurately reflect non-Indigenous experiences.

A constant theme throughout the anthology revolves around Indigenous identity: Who gets to define it and how it is operationalized for data collection? Chapters 8, 9, and 12 explicitly explore the importance of the answers to these questions in Basque Country, Mexico, and Colombia. In the case of Basque Country in Spain, the question of Indigeneity is framed against that of a minority population, while exploring the power of data to shape public perception. Meanwhile, chapters 9 and 12 focus on ways of defining "Indigenous." Mexico uses physical features, culture, and the sense of community to define individuals as Indigenous, whereas Colombia's definitions originate from transitional justice tribunal rulings.

Another valuable element of the collection is the repeated demonstration that the mining of Indigenous data by non-Indigenous nations is just the most recent example of colonial powers extracting resources from Indigenous People, communities, and nations. Making this connection helps detach the common misperception that data merely demonstrate objective facts and establishes that at best the current social construction of data prioritizes the needs of dominant society at the expense of Indigenous People.

The volume serves as an important resource for those looking to understand the Indigenous data sovereignty movement; the need for a more inclusive process for data creation; and current best practices for partnering with Indigenous nations to create data that actually serves the needs of Indigenous People. The chapters take an interdisciplinary approach to the topic and are accessible to undergraduates taking their first class in Indigenous studies but are also varied and detailed enough to also benefit higher-level students.

JEFFREY D. BURNETTE is assistant professor in the Department of Sociology and Anthropology at Rochester Institute of Technology.

# THEODORE C. VAN ALST JR.

*Velroy and the Madischie Mafia*
by Sy Hoahwah
University of New Mexico Press, 2021

THERE'S SOMETHING THAT HAPPENS in Urban Native lit: it's a way of talking, of working the story. It happens in flashes, brief lights and inky voids, illuminations and absences: all necessary to tell tales that don't take place on long, lonely roads or across open fields where the sun can set endlessly in a slow dance with the reader. There is one exception, though; a ruralish and decidedly Western scene that enters, no matter how big or small the cityscape: the canyon. Walls and buildings, courts and chasms all make canyons in the city, even if it's small-town public housing. The protection and confinement and the safety and limitations of that kind of space weigh in on the walker there.

The rolling runs into the roiling in "Red River," where at Yellow House Canyon, "Tonkawa scouts cannibalistically count out / a bag of children's hands" (37). Hoahwah navigates these spaces deftly and skillfully. The psychogeographic influence of SW Oklahoma on Velroy and crew relate directly to the land's temporal evolution; the two lines cross back and forth between the poems as they work to draw each other back from a sketch to a clear figure of contemporary *urbandigineity*, a word I haven't seen before but one I find myself needing here. Velroy and his crew constitute a necessary *dérive*, a ranging patrol of watchful eyes to mark passages in and out of their territory—places that need them as much as they need it. An elucidation perhaps, via Guy Debord's unverifiable quote of Marx in the 1959 film *Sur le passage de quelques personnes à travers une assez courte unité de temps* (On the passage of a few people through a relatively short period): "People can see nothing around them that is not their own image; everything speaks to them of themselves. Their very landscape is animated. Obstacles were everywhere. And they were all interrelated, maintaining a unified reign of poverty." It is in this last line that Hoahwah's transgressions are made clear—the only poverty extant is what Americans might imagine has happened to their former foes on the southern plains. While Western markers of success and wealth might be pursued in bits and pieces by the players, the richness of the lands that embrace them, even if a bit tightly at times, are described in haunting, dramatic, and sharply historical images that animate the present. Battles rage through the years; timeless divinations and quests animate the pages such as those in "Account of the Lost Valley Fight, 1873." Figures lurch from the deep dark in nightmarish ways made comforting and laced with love:

> In honor, Kot-see was seated up in the saddle,
> tied down at the wrists.
> By pulling on the ropes from time to time
> members of the Black Knife Society
> balanced his tattered body.
> His forehead touched the sky,
> gunshot face leaked worms. (11)

This review is one of many as this collection was first published in 2009. A couple of my colleagues have written about it in other places. I didn't know this when I agreed to the review; yet after having read this work a few times, I can see why the University of New Mexico Press has rereleased it. It's powerful, important, and timely in the way that poetry can be, urgent in the current movement of Native literary work from urban spaces. Hoahwah has given us a work that shines through time, constantly reminding us that we, along with he and the "traceless descendants of the Black Knife Society" in his final offering, "Alight," "quietly listen / For our language, hungry to answer" (52).

And though Debord was later critiquing cinema in that same film, he made a point worth pondering in the dark as we close: "Stars are created by the need we have for them." Rural or urban, the night canyon you might find yourself in the bottom of demands words of light like Hoahwah's to weave the glow we need to see our way out.

THEODORE C. VAN ALST JR. is an enrolled member of Mackinac Bands of Chippewa and Ottawa Indians. He is the chair and Tilikum Professor of Indigenous Nations Studies at Portland State University.

# JOSEPH M. PIERCE

*The Conquest of the Desert: Argentina's Indigenous Peoples
    and the Battle for History*
edited by Carolyne R. Larson
University of New Mexico Press, 2020

SOME EVENTS IN HISTORY seem to take on a life of their own. Often born of violence, these moments exceed chronology and themselves become orienting devices with a narrative magnetism that is difficult to escape (i.e., 1492). In Argentine history, the so-called Conquista del Desierto (Conquest of the Desert) is one such event, a campaign of military, economic, and territorial occupation of Indigenous land that took place in the 1870s and 1880s as part of the expansion of the settler colonial nation-state toward what it now calls the "Patagonia" or the "south of Argentina."

Carolyne R. Larson's edited volume, *The Conquest of the Desert: Argentina's Indigenous Peoples and the Battle for History*, attempts to expand the possibilities of interpreting this campaign beyond canonical historiography and toward multiple, interdisciplinary frames of reference. Divided into an introduction and nine chapters, the contributors include experts on nation formation, memory studies, genocide studies, environmentalism, literature and culture, and sociology. I appreciate how the volume not only questions academic disciplines but also the circulation of knowledge "about" history and the concomitant privileging of U.S.-based academics and scholarship. The book models how a singular topic, in this case the Conquista del Desierto, can be pried open, reassembled, and reimagined across territories, languages, and academic fields.

For a project that claims to be invested in questioning historiographical praxis, this study oddly does not include the voices of Indigenous Peoples themselves. To my knowledge there are no Indigenous contributors to this volume. What is more, there is no recognition of this lack or the erasure that it perpetuates. It is one thing to say that history needs to be reevaluated considering a new set of methodological tools, but it is quite another to presume to tell the story of the Conquista del Desierto without the inclusion of the "conquered" themselves. While the editor's introduction claims that the book "highlights indigenous and other counternarratives that challenge the official stories about the conquest," (2) Indigenous voices are largely absent from this narration, and the epistemological framing of "conquest"—and of history as a battle—limits the intervention that this work could have made.

Take the arresting photograph that adorns the cover. No contributor analyzes it, and the subjects photographed remain nameless, as does the territory in which it was taken. We are only informed that the image was sourced from the Museo Etnográfico Juan B. Ambrosetti, part of the University of Buenos Aires. This gap is symptomatic of the edited volume and its framing of history. Yes, Indians appear, but their voices, names, feelings, and lives are registered only as background and as part of a disputed past that somehow never manages to include them. While the introduction promises to trouble disciplinary boundaries by looking "through the lenses of indigenous perspectives," (11) none of those perspectives speak in their own voice or on their own terms.

Individual chapters take up literary representation (Jennie I. Daniels), the sequestering and display of live Indigenous People in museums (Ricardo D. Salvatore), the negotiations between Mapuche and Tehuelche leaders in combat (Julio Vezub and Mark Healey), environmental and meteorological influences on the outcome of the "conquest" (Rob Christensen), and the discursive harnessing of the nineteenth-century military campaign by the leaders of Argentina's last military dictatorship (1976–1983) (David M. K. Sheinin). While as a whole the collection challenges the legitimacy of the dominant historical archive, it nevertheless renders static certain frames of reference—in particular those related to orality, affect, and memory.

Notable exceptions include the chapter by Walter Delrio and Pilar Pérez that emerged from the collective work of the Network of Researchers on Genocide and Indigenous Politics in Argentina, and the final two chapters, both of which engage in a reading of Mapuche cultural production that allows the community itself to come to the fore. Ana Ramos provides a sensitive reading of Mapuche memory, focusing on the collective telling of *nütram,* a discursive rendering of history as lived, recounted, and felt across time. Sarah D. Warren's chapter takes up contemporary imaginaries of territory, forms of claiming territorial coherence through community-based art, and political praxis—in particular mapmaking—in a way that engages with the internal logics of Mapuche history. The history of this, like other "conquests," deserves to be critiqued and reimagined, but it is imperative that the praxis of history be told from within (rather than without) Indigenous epistemologies. The voices of Indigenous Peoples themselves deserve to tell this history.

JOSEPH M. PIERCE (Cherokee Nation citizen) is associate professor in the Department of Hispanic Languages and Literature at Stony Brook University.

# STERLING FLUHARTY

*Teaching Native Pride: Upward Bound and the Legacy of Isabel Bond*
by Tony Tekaroniake Evans
Washington State University Press, 2021

**IN THE EARLY 1970S** Isabel Bond became director of the Upward Bound program at the University of Idaho. The six-week summer program, born out of the War on Poverty, primarily served low-income and at-risk high school students from families whose members had never attended college. The university campus was in Moscow, Idaho, between the Coeur d'Alene and Nez Perce reservations. During the program's initial decades, high school students had to live within two hundred miles of the campus to be eligible, which meant a high proportion of participants were tribal members. Over three decades, Bond worked tirelessly to get more than two thousand participants ready for college.

Bond had deep roots in Idaho that intertwined with its Native residents. Her grandparents arrived in the state in the late 1800s to farm a homestead. Around the same time, Chief Joseph and his people lost their homelands in the Nez Perce War. Bond was born in 1932 to an accomplished mother who devoted her life to community service. Bond was also influenced by an uncle who made Native friends and picked up the tribal language while living and working on the Nez Perce reservation. Her uncle was good friends with Jackson Sundown, a nephew of Chief Joseph who won the World Saddle Bronc Championship at the 1916 Pendleton Round-Up. "Rodeo judges were not inclined to give credit to an Indian rider at the time," a cousin of Bond's recalled, "but the crowd went crazy at them when they tried to ignore his performance" (59).

When Ed Madsen, a Nez Perce schoolteacher, launched Upward Bound at the University of Idaho, Native and white children in the area attended segregated schools. Otis Halfmoon was one of the first Nez Perce students to enroll in Madsen's program. In those early days on campus, Halfmoon remembered, "Non-Indian kids would drive by whopping at us, yelling for us to go back to the reservation, but this only caused us to stick together, white students and Indian students. We were all Upward Bound students" (22). Madsen balanced academics and study skills with Indian culture and organized a powwow in the summer of 1969 that brought tribal families from nearby reservations to the campus. "Pride was one of the main things he instilled in us," Halfmoon recalled. "We learned that education is the answer. We had a choice: to either become educated and be equal to the white man or become his subject" (22).

In early 1969, Madsen hired Bond to teach home economics to the Upward Bound students. Bond had moved back to Moscow the year before, when the university hired her husband as a geology professor. Bond taught the participants in Madsen's program how to make vests, which they then wore as regalia during the powwow that summer. While working with the students, Bond traveled to their homes, became acquainted with their relatives, and witnessed the kinds of challenges they faced in their communities. This work rekindled memories of the Nez Perce individuals and culture her uncle had brought to her mother's farm. "It just all started coming back when I started working these kids," Bond recalled (30–31). After Madsen passed away in 1972, the dean of the education college appointed Bond director of Upward Bound the following year.

Bill Picard was one of the Nez Perce students who attended Bond's Upward Bound program in the 1970s. Before entering the program, he spent his summers working as a farm laborer. "One day, a teacher advised me to learn the job well, because Indians don't go to college," he recalled (45). When Picard enrolled in Upward Bound, he found a different attitude. "Isabel was the first person who ever told me that I was capable of achieving something," he remembered. "Even now, she says I should go get a master's degree. Isabel was more of an auntie than a teacher" (46). Decades later, Picard was serving on the Nez Perce Executive Committee and attending an educational conference when he ran into the first teacher. "He said that I was the last person he ever expected to see at such a conference," Picard recalled (46).

After Bond stepped down from the Upward Bound program in 2006, she began teaching at the Northwest Indian College campus in Lapwai, where Picard served as site manager. "After you read this book, you will know that Isabel Bond is a very special person, the kind you only come across once in a lifetime," Picard wrote in the forward to this book (x).

**STERLING FLUHARTY** is an independent scholar.

# SHANNA KETCHUM-HEAP OF BIRDS

*Painting Culture, Painting Nature: Stephen Mopope, Oscar Jacobson,*
    *and the Development of Indian Art in Oklahoma*
by Gunlög Fur
University of Oklahoma Press, 2019

GUNLÖG FUR DESCRIBES *Painting Culture, Painting Nature* as an attempt to "present aspects of the concurrent lives of immigrants and Indians in Oklahoma," (6) namely, Swedish-born art professor Oscar Brousse Jacobson (1882–1966) and Kiowa painter, dancer, and musician Stephen Mopope (1898–1974). Fur presents both men as visionary figures who, together, transformed Oklahoma into the center of exciting new developments in Indian art in the late 1920s. Fur focuses on Mopope as a student of Jacobson, but he and the other Kiowa artists (Spencer Asah, James Auchiah, Lois Bougetah Smoky, Jack Hokeah, and Monroe Tsatoke)—collectively known as the Kiowa Five or Six—and their families are approached through their entanglements with the Jacobson family and their circle of contacts in order to "investigate a relationship that cut across social, cultural, and racial divide[s]" (5).

By contending that Indians and immigrants mixed in the land of the red earth (or Oklahoma) Fur challenges Euro-American modernist discourse that presumed a fundamental difference between "primitive" and "modern" (4) peoples. By drawing on postcolonial methodologies such as concurrences and diasporas to challenge the universality of historical claims, Fur sets the stage brilliantly to "frame the conditions of the encounter between Mopope and Jacobson [as an] individual and collective search for identification among both Kiowas and Swedes" (27) in the United States at the turn of the twentieth century. The argument is tricky because, on the one hand, narrating the parallel and divergent lives of Mopope and Jacobson rightly asserts what Native American scholar Phil Deloria calls a "study of where Indians are allowed to be placed [. . .] as particip[ants] in the production of modern discourse—and of modernity itself" (10).

On the other hand, postcolonial theories of migration do not apply well in Native American contexts because of the process of settler colonialism. The use of a diasporic perspective focused on mobility marks Mopope and Jacobson differently because, as Fur states, "Swedish immigrants became intricately involved in a process of settler colonialism that ultimately dispossessed American Indian peoples of land, culture, and language" (7). Fur is aware of asymmetrical power relations but does not go beyond the shortcomings of postcolonial theoretical paradigms to critically analyze art historical narratives that privilege the development of American national identity and history. Even though influential art historians in the field of Native American, or Indigenous, art, such as Ruth Phillips, Janet C. Berlo, and Elizabeth Hutchinson are mentioned, Fur is careful to admit that the book is focused only on Mopope's experiences as opposed to the Kiowa Five or Six group to which he belonged and not on "the objects themselves but on the artists and their locations" (18).

Fur's focus on one male member of the Kiowa Six (even though one Kiowa female, Lois Bougetah Smoky, was a member) and the use of colonial archives, records, and recordings to explain the friendship between Mopope and Jacobson means an opportunity lost to truly explore why both men's artistic subjects and styles diverged. Fur contends that nostalgia inspired Jacobson to paint landscapes of the West, uninfluenced by human activity, and Mopope to represent Kiowa life and history in his art because both were modern and compatible in their mutual accomplishments. One would hope that, despite their personal expressions, future studies of the Kiowa Six and Jacobson will embrace a decolonial perspective that considers the critical connections between painting nature and culture, or history and identity, within the framework of art history and criticism. Only then will the work of art historian Laura E. Smith—on the Kiowa photographer Horace Poolaw—and the oral stories told by Vanessa Paukeigope Jennings, granddaughter of Stephen Mopope, begin to transmit decades of Native scholarship that survived the brutal history of Oklahoma statehood and Native relationships with European immigrants.

**SHANNA KETCHUM-HEAP OF BIRDS** (Diné/Navajo Nation) holds a Ph.D. from the University of Middlesex, London, England.

# CAMILLA TOWNSEND

*Cacicas: The Indigenous Women Leaders of Spanish America, 1492–1825*
edited by Margarita R. Ochoa and Sara Vicuña Guengerich
University of Oklahoma Press, 2021

**IN THE CONCLUDING COMMENTS** in this fine new edited collection, Mónica Díaz suggests that we should sometimes relinquish our scholarly need to prove that we are changing paradigms and simply "appreciate the changes that have occurred in our disciplines and celebrate important milestones" (269). The pieces in this anthology are uniformly excellent, reminding us how far the study of Native American women has come in the past thirty years.

Ida Altman opens the volume with a prologue on female political leaders recognized by the Spaniards in the early Caribbean; then the editors Ochoa and Guengerich provide a thorough introduction to the subject of women leaders in mainland Spanish America in the context of Indigenous nobility in general. They acknowledge that the term "cacica" was a Spanish invention (feminizing *cacique,* the Arawak word for "chief") and that women most often did not hold formal political power either in preconquest America or after the Spanish incursion. The editors and authors encourage the study of women's interventions in the public arena through other means. Most of the evidence comes from Native women's active participation in the extensive litigation in the Spanish American world. The volume consists of two sets of essays, the first on Mesoamerica (with contributing authors Brad Benton, Peter Villella, Margarita Ochoa, and Catherine Komisaruk), and the second on South America (including authors Karen Graubart, Chantal Caillavet, Liliana Pérez together with Renzo Honores, Sara Guengerich, and Florencia Roulet). At nearly every turn, the authors argue that cacicas used the tools at their disposal to influence events around them. The most common theme is that they used Spanish law to carve out increasing power for themselves.

To my mind, the book begs two sets of questions, calling out for further analysis in two arenas: First, how might we put what we know about Indigenous women leaders in Spanish America in conversation with what we know about North America? Second, is it possible that we are going too far in our search for women's power and consequently overlooking evidence of devastating loss?

Comparisons with North America come to mind numerous times. When

Roulet writes about "Peacemaker Cacicas in the Río de la Plata Southern Frontier," one is struck by the close parallels not only with Julianna Barr's work (which the author mentions) but also with nearly every other study of women in peripheral middle grounds. When Peter Villella writes about the "Founding Mothers" of Querétaro in his piece on the Otomí women whose husbands and brothers allied with an early arriving Spaniard to form a frontier trade empire, one thinks repeatedly of the literature on the fur trade and the establishment of wealthy Métis families.

All the essays provide food for thought on the eternal conundrum of how to weigh both power and loss at the same time. The volume offers a rather relentless focus on empowerment, even on occasions when the evidence leads this reader, at least, to see enforced limitation. The essays by Komisaruk and Graubart come as something of a relief in this regard, as they speak directly to questions others choose to ignore. Komisaruk, for instance, reminds readers that over the course of the colonial era, Indigenous nobles lost the power that had belonged to their family by right of tradition; instead, Native people learned to take power through their access to political positions or to certain trades. But women were excluded from both; over time, their power became more tenuous. She trenchantly observes, for instance, that one "ex-gobernadora" (the widow of an Indigenous gobernador, head of a local cabildo) in Guatemala lived in penury; her grandson worked as a day laborer. Graubart shows how Indigenous women in Peru made strategic use of arguments that Spanish courts would accept in their quest to have themselves named to political positions that probably would not have been theirs before the conquest; she also demonstrates that their cases were most successful when they had personal connections to Spanish society. The evidence proves the brilliance of certain women's thinking as well as the need for luck; it does not demonstrate the continuing power of cacicas, much less of Native women in general.

*Cacicas* is truly a joy, offering such rich evidence that readers are able to grapple with large questions and even form their own conclusions.

CAMILLA TOWNSEND is distinguished professor of history at Rutgers University.

# ALEX RED CORN

*Sharice's Big Voice: A Native Kid Becomes a Congresswoman*
by Sharice Davids (with Nancy K. Mays), illustrated by Joshua Mangeshig
   Pawis-Steckley
HarperCollins, 2021

**WHEN READING** *Sharice's Big Voice: A Native Kid Becomes a Congresswoman*, I was taking in the moment of everything this book represents for me and my family. Politics aside, as an Osage living in Congresswoman Davids' district, I was proud to read this book and show it to my children. For me, this story represents the first time a Native person has been on my ballot in a non-tribal election. Beyond that, this story is an important contribution to children's literature.

Refreshingly, the book resists the typical trappings found in children's books about Indigenous Peoples, giving me confidence that publishers are paying attention to important nuances about Native representation in media, curricula, and learning materials. As Congresswoman Davids (along with Kathy Mays and Wasauksing artist Joshua Mangeshig Pawis-Steckley) reveals about her journey from childhood to her congressional election, she pushes back against the oversimplified stuck-in-the-past exotic Indian stereotypes that are problematic for children's learning. This book focuses on a positive message about the importance of listening and learning, hard work, and tenacity, all through the unique and layered sociocultural lens of her life.

Within Davids' story, you see an energetic Ho-Chunk child raised by her hardworking mother and role model (who becomes a Sergeant first class in the Army). As a child, Congresswoman Davids characterizes herself as talkative with a "big voice," connecting to how Ho-Chunk people refer to themselves: "The People of the Big Voice" (8). As a girl, Davids describes her desire to emulate Bruce Lee's "punching" and "kicking," showing a strong young girl who builds her physical and mental strength to eventually become an accomplished woman (10). Davids tells of emulating the "hard work" that she witnessed from her mother, who taught her how to be "focused and fierce," yet also "confident and kind" while working in the service of others (12). The Congresswoman's message of strength and perseverance is central as she describes young adulthood experiences in law school, her early law career in a big firm as well as on reservations, and eventually working in the

White House. As the story evolves, a message about representation emerges as she describes how in many of the places she worked, few people were like her, and there was a need for more diverse voices to be heard when making laws. The need for diversity motivated her to run for office and also influenced her successful election campaign, which focused on bringing a diverse group of people together to accomplish shared goals.

These core themes are clearly important contributions to children's literature. However, what's most refreshing about this book is how these themes are delivered: through the lens of an accomplished modern Native woman from the LGBTQ community who has a big personality, big ideas, and a big future. *Sharice's Big Voice* allows Native children to see a more accurate version of their potential futures. Even better, the attractive illustrations enable readers to see beyond the old sepia-toned media stereotypes that have historically dominated the image of who Native people are and who they can be.

The final pages feature personal notes from the author and illustrator, which are important additions for those reading this book to children. In these sections, you can read about how they find solidarity and shared experiences of resiliency while growing up disconnected from their affiliated nations, as well as the value of being able to access stories about Two-Spirit Natives. The final section, written by John Greendeer (former president of the Ho-Chunk Nation), offers cultural context connecting Congresswoman Davids's story with Ho-Chunk (and Winnebago) histories. Greendeer's message is an important part of the book in terms of Indigenous self-determination and intellectual sovereignty, even if not framed in those terms. In other words, the book doesn't just carry a message about representation: the concept appears to have been prioritized during its construction. While I am unaware of who reviewed or advised on the book, it appears that Congresswoman Davids' and Ho-Chunk perspectives were important priorities throughout the process, which makes me like this book even more.

In conclusion, Davids's book is important not just for me and my family but for all families looking for up-to-date stories about Indigenous experiences in our society.

**ALEX RED CORN** (ʰʌ ʒʌ ʒɑ/Osage) is assistant professor of educational leadership in the College of Education at Kansas State University.

# ARTURO ARIAS

*Le Maya Q'atzij /Our Maya Word: Poetics of Resistance in Guatemala*
by Emil Keme'
University of Minnesota Press, 2021

**LE MAYA Q'ATZIJ/OUR MAYA WORD** constitutes a truly original effort to conceptualize contemporary Guatemalan Maya literary production. Keme' develops a methodological and theoretical foundation to argue that, in the recent abundance of published poetry, Guatemala's Maya writers are reinscribing their cultural memory. They make sense of the past and engage in multilayered discussions about their present and future beingness and development in their native territories. Keme' analyzes three distinct historical phases during which Maya authors engaged with the violent legacies of military dictatorships to produce powerful new works. These texts broadened debates on the possibilities and limits of a politics of recognition in their racialized struggles against the country's elite Mestizo population.

Keme' argues that traditional ontological elements of Maya culture are reconfigured discursively by the poets he examines to reshape social meanings, whether in their struggles against military genocide, heterosexist violence, or extractive destruction of the environment.

Keme' has ordered his work historically, beginning with the earliest Maya poets who published their works in the early 1960s, then moving on to the most recent luminaries appearing on the poetic landscape. He often selects one or two poems from each author to perform an in-depth analysis of their meaning and vision. In this logic, the first chapter of *Maya Q'atzij* opens with the forerunners of this movement: Kaqchikel poets Francisco Morales Santos and Luis de Lión. Keme' focuses on Morales Santos's poem "Volveremos" (We will return) from *Agua en el silencio* (1961; Water in silence), which the author sees as the first contemporary Maya literary manifesto (a point with which I concur). He then turns to *Madre, nosotros también somos historia* (1988; Mother, we too are history) to broaden the depth of Santos's production. From De Lión he focuses on *Poemas del volcán de agua, los poemas míos* (1991; Poems from the Agua Volcano, my poems).

Keme' states that Morales Santos's journey expresses a critique of modernity and its hegemonic narratives: most particularly the official historiography that justified the plundering of Maya lands and culture in the name of Eurocentric modernity. He sees Morales Santos as crafting a mental and political process of de-alienation for readers of Guatemalan Maya origin, much like himself, who originally fled from their racialized identity and Maya roots and then belatedly returned to them.

Chapter 2 focuses on *Ajyuq'/El animalero* (1990; Many animals) by Maya K'iche' poet Humberto Ak'abal, *Piedras labradas/Sculpted Stones* (1995) by Maya Pop'ti Victor Montejo, and *Sq'anej maya'/Palabras mayas* (1998; Maya words) by Q'anjob'al author Gaspar Pedro Gonzalez. Keme' understands these authors as performing testimonial poetry against state terrorism. Poetic meter and chiasmus are problematized among other traits—something always critically important in books analyzing poetry. González is rendered as a bearer of memory, Ak'abal as performing lexical estrangement. All three establish the basis for an epistemological struggle in which, by transfiguring their lived experiences, other Maya voices may become empowered, thus legitimizing their world culturally and politically.

Chapter 3 explores a new generation of Guatemalan Maya poets, represented by K'iche'/Kaqchikel Rosa Chávez, K'iche' Pablo Garcia, and Q'anjob'al Sabino Esteban Francisco. In Keme's understanding, this generation contests their predecessors' stand by exploring new topics emerging in the aftermath of the Guatemalan Civil War: from the consequences of globalization to migration, or the role gender plays in Maya communities. In Keme's understanding, the metaphor of the journey to the underworld enables their work to provide both a critique and a demystification of Guatemalan narratives of citizenship and nationhood.

In his last chapter, Keme' turns to feminist and queer issues by looking at the works of Maya Cu Choc and Manuel Tzoc. He states that Cu Choc breaks with theoretical presuppositions that Maya cultures were dependent on orality. As for Tzoc, Keme' understands *Gay(o)* as a critique of brutal heteronormative politics imposed by the state. Tzoc's defiance generates in his eyes an erotics of sovereignty. This chapter may very well be the most original in the book.

Keme's nuanced reading of these authors enriches our understanding of Maya poetry. *Maya Q'atzij* weaves poetic analysis, probes sociopolitical issues, and offers a historical perusal of Guatemala's Mayas. Keme' has produced a major work that will enrich all those who read it.

**ARTURO ARIAS** is John D. and Catherine T. MacArthur Foundation Professor in the Humanities at the University of California, Merced.

# HAGWIL HAYETSK (CHARLES R. MENZIES)

*Shaping the Future on Haida Gwaii: Life beyond Settler Colonialism*
by Joseph Weiss
UBC Press, 2019

WEISS ARRIVED IN HAIDA GWAI with the weight of dead generations of settler anthropologists before him. These sojourners were drawn to the oceanic Haida homeland. After visiting, the anthropologists returned home with chests and minds filled with the memorabilia of their visits. They proceeded to write books that spoke to audiences in metropolitan centers of colonialism. Weiss is part of this tradition, though he also speaks from a place that is as much concerned with Indigenous subjects as with the settlers' own implications within colonialism. It's a new kind of permission-seeking anthropology that tries to be less controlling.

Weis is at pains to show he is not imposing himself upon Haida people. We learn clues, for example, about how Weiss navigated permission in his acknowledgments (xi–x) where he thanks (using the Haida word) the communities of Old Masset and Masset: "And first among firsts, I am grateful to Agnes Davis and her family. I learned the Haida word for thank you, *how.aa*, sitting at Noonie Aggie's kitchen table, and she [and family] . . . were my first hosts in Old Massett" (xi). Later Weiss thanks the formal governance structures of the Haida Nation (x). There is no clear foregrounding of how permission was obtained—but we know that it was indeed granted. This is a common thread in current ethnographies. Authors paint their authenticity and sincerity through measured inclusions—such as the challenge from "Lauren" that Weiss faced (see pp. 21–25): "What makes you different from all the others who have come and gone?" Lauren asks. Weiss doesn't really tell us, but he clearly leaves the impression he is different; I would have to agree—he is trying hard to apply the lessons Indigenous Peoples have been trying to teach settlers: respect us as we are; don't tell us what we should be; and pay attention to who we are as real people present in our own worlds.

I share a space with Weiss as an anthropologist. I share a space with Haida as an Indigenous person. My own Gitxaała family links me to Haida people. I share an understanding of "home" in the same manner that Weiss describes for the Haida (63–90). As a Gitxaała person I have witnessed settler sojourners passing through our *laxyuup* (territory/home). As an Indigenous person

I am of mixed minds when I read works like *Shaping the Future on Haida Gwaii*. This book is certainly no Evans Pritchard ethnography in which *The People* are marched into the ethnographer's tent from their refugee camp to answer his questions. Yet the agenda remains driven by concerns, forces, and theories arising from the settler's world; it still responds to questions the settler is asking. Where is attention paid to the authority and jurisdiction of the *sm'gygyet* (hereditary leadership)? The anthropologist asks for permission, but what are the conditions under which this permission is granted? This is not a critique of how individual anthropologists build respect and rapport but rather an interrogation of the wider context within which individuals maneuver as they seek permission.

The strength of the book is its focus on Indigenous futures. Futures here are used to examine what people, specifically Haida, are doing to actively engage and shape their world. Set against a disciplinary history of chronicling the "disappearing Indian" and settler state actions to ensure "Indians" did disappear, Weiss listens to the different Haida voices that speak to existing Haida conceptions of where they are going. Weiss listens carefully to his Haida interlocuters and accepts that there is more than one Haida act of future making. This is important, especially in a discipline (anthropology) so strongly influenced by Eurocentric Durkheimian thinking. What might, perhaps, link the rich diversity of future making is how it is "a way of thinking [and, I would suggest, acting] out from within the temporal brackets of settler colonialism's" acts of disappearing "the Indian" (183).

*Shaping the Future* is erudite, sensitive, informed, and relevant. It is everything that one might ask for in a new-times anthropology book. Weiss is aware of his subjective location. He is cautious in making overclaims. He does not simplify Haida people into *the Haida*. I would recommend this book to everyone. At the same time, I realize I would rather be reading a book by a Haida author even if this settler author has given us one so sensitively and carefully done as *Shaping the Future*.

HAGWIL HAYETSK (CHARLES R. MENZIES) is a member of Gitxaała Nation and a faculty member at the University of British Columbia.

# LIZA GRANDIA

*Indigenous Food Systems: Concepts, Cases, and Conversations*
edited by Priscilla Settee and Shailesh Shukla
Canadian Scholars, 2020

IN 1996, seventy organizations representing peasant, Indigenous, fisherfolk, farmworker, and other land-based movements from six continents gathered in Tlaxcala, Mexico, for the second international conference organized by Via Campesina (translated in English as "the peasant way"). Countering the caloric-centric rhetoric of "food security" from the Cold War era, Via Campesina delegates proclaimed core principles of "food sovereignty" to support the rights of small food producers to control land, water, and natural resources. The language of sovereignty appealed to many impoverished nations who had begun to question unfair World Trade Organization rules on agriculture and also resonated with North American tribal governments for whom the concept underscores their inherent right to self-determination.

With agribusiness giants merging into just three global conglomerates in the 2000–2010s, the defense of seeds from patents or genetic modification rightly became a global mobilizing issue for Via Campesina, which now represents 200 million families from 182 organizations. Not all small producers plant seeds, however. While some of Turtle Island was agrarian (and on par with other great agricultural civilizations in Mesopotamia and China), two-thirds of North America's Original Peoples relied on seasonal hunting, fishing, and gathering. The wild rice, berries, meat, and medicines of First Nations/ Inuit/Métis food systems of the far North, by necessity, are stewarded collectively and transgenerationally. As one author aptly put it, "Asatiwisipe Anishinaabeg food sovereignty needs a community to feed a community" (63). Health itself in Cree is *miyupimaatisiiun* ("being alive [together] well" [89]).

Emphasizing this fundamental point in multiple ways, this marvelous volume is organized into three parts: a conceptual introduction, community cases, and final reflections for action. Readers should sample the dessert first—that is, the final editorial synthesis (chapter 15)—then delve backward through the cases and chew last on the theoretical chapters (if their digestion can handle the "phenomenological" dressing). For use as a textbook, each chapter has an outline, definitions, role models in the author biographies, and brilliant pedagogical questions for broader critical thinking.

On average, a third of Canada's Indigenous Peoples are food insecure.

Rather than approaching the topic from deficit-based questions of "lack," hunger, and poverty, the authors document and make visible the quiet but consequential ways that Indigenous Peoples remain resiliently committed to harvesting, bartering, and sharing land/bush/country food—even across long distances with their urban kinfolk (chapter 10). While corporate billionaires seek prestige with phallic space rockets, First Nations subsistence systems display a truer form of affluence, where "the hunter who is generous with the products of his harvest is usually one of the most influential men in the community" (66, from chapter 4 on Anishinaabe customary laws, wildlife knowledge, and trapping practices). For subsistence producers, territory is simultaneously foodscape, landscape, and culturescape through blood memory. Ancestral bush skills of seasonal and long-term planning are also plain hard work—and "to be alone in the still silence of the wilderness is not easy to master" (58).

Bureaucratic systems can never capture the intricate web of social and ecological relations needed to survive on the land, so subsistence providers face innumerable institutional obstacles in acquiring hunting, harvesting, and firearm permits to continue millennial practices in their own territory. Although the settler fur trade caused the near extinction of key wildlife species (e.g., beaver, bison, wolf) that served as "ecosystem engineers," the Northern Store (*directly* descended from two British colonial companies) continues to enjoy a retail monopoly in many remote towns, charging outrageous prices for subsidized junk food. Even while Indigenous advocates have successfully begun to decolonize Canada's Food Guide to include "nutritious traditional foods" in the food pyramid, other public health regulations perversely force traditional foods underground. Chuckling at the absurdity of settler "help," one Elder reflected on how "someone from Winnipeg" decided to send a northern First Nation some cows that promptly got eaten by wolves (73).

With gentle critique of the agrarian bias of the global food sovereignty movement, this anthology will, of course, be of interest to Canadian Indigenous studies but also to allied scholars/practitioners/movements for climate resilience and food sustainability. With industrial food and meat systems contributing to at least one third of global heating, texts like this offer vital living ideas for regenerative food systems that symbiotically can reduce carbon emissions. All the authors were impressively attentive to relationships, respect, and reciprocity—with many proactively engaged with creative working groups, town, tribal, and even international initiatives for food justice. They illustrate that food sovereignty is "not something you ask for" or just write about but rather "something you do" (108).

LIZA GRANDIA is associate professor of Native American studies at the University of California, Davis.

# CLEMENTINE BORDEAUX

*Honor Thy Mother: The Untold Story of Aboriginal Women and their Indipino Children*
by Lucy Ostrander
Stourwater Pictures

**THE 2021 FILM** *Honor Thy Mother* opens with a brief explanation of Aboriginal boarding school history. Like most documentaries about boarding and residential school history, the film utilizes old photographs of children juxtaposed against stark images of priests and nuns. A quick internet search of "aboriginal boarding schools" yields about 29,900,000 results. The image search produces black-and-white images of school-age Indigenous children sitting outside residential schools, or comparison photos of pre—boarding school versus post—boarding school. Any student or scholar of boarding school history has seen these photos used to demonstrate the atrocities at these institutions.

At an initial glance, the documentary film seemed to be engaging in a typical story of the boarding school experience. The tie between historical trauma and residential schools in North America has been explored in many fictional and nonfictional films. However, Lucy Ostrander and Stourwater Pictures take the audience through a nuanced account of the descendants of Northwest coastal women who ended up in Bainbridge Island in the 1940s. After being removed from their tribal homes and placed in boarding schools, these women found work and love. Through oral histories and archival material, we witness their journeys from residential schools to building families with Filipino farmworkers and raising children while hiding their indigeneity. The film addresses a complicated history that is difficult to unpack in just one movie.

The documentary utilizes the voices of children of a variety of Indigenous women and Filipino immigrant workers. Now Elders, these children consider themselves "Indipinos" and deliver emotional accounts of being raised within impoverished and racially charged spaces. The children, as adults, share the perplexity of being presented with a limited sense of Indigenous kinship or Filipino culture. The "Indipino" children struggled to live within "white standards," resulting in a feeling of invisibility and misunderstandings. The Indipino Elders share deeply impactful narratives of emotional survival and the ways they had to navigate the invisibility of their mothers.

Their confusion of belonging draws into focus the ongoing incursion of settler colonialism. The intersection of settler colonialism, imperialism, and capitalism brings into focus the experiences of the women who survived Indian residential school and their descendants. The film echoes the continued erasure of Indigenous histories and kinship while also reminding us of the legacy of labor and dispossession. The experiences shared in the film are integral to sharing stories of intergenerational trauma that continues today. Indipino stories are important to unpacking the difficult conversations needed to better understand specific impacts on the Northwest Coast.

The film provides insight into significant intersections between women who survived Indian residential schools, immigrant workers, and the influence of land. Although being forced from their homelands, these women raised families on the shores of the Salish Sea. Their children eventually found their way back to their Indigenous heritage while honoring their Indipino identities. Through their narratives, they demonstrate the crucial intersections of Northwest Coast histories. The film is a moving tribute to the many Indigenous mothers that found kinship on Bainbridge Island and built a community to honor their ancestry.

*Honor Thy Mother* would be a valuable addition to any course addressing the long-lasting impact of the harms of colonialism, especially on the Northwest Coast. The film utilized beautiful and generous first-person accounts alongside in-depth archival research. The film also follows a typical Western-style documentary approach. Unlike the recent experimental documentary film work of artists such as Sky Hopinka or Marcella Ernest, the film aligns well with an expected linear outcome in a short documentary.

The film exposes the legacies of colonial disparities that are hyperfocused on specific communities without creating more invisibility. I was excited to experience a regionally concentrated story about the legacies of boarding and residential schools. The inclusion of the Kitsap community provides a way to map issues in a unique time and space that directly impacts Bainbridge Island, the Salish Sea, and the Northwest Coast. Aside from the opening scenes, images and interviews are concentrated on the people of these communities.

The film is poignant and timely. The past decade of documentary film has led to a specificity that recognizes the complexities of reclaiming indigeneity. *Honor Thy Mother* reminds us that we also can celebrate the interconnectedness of gender and race. Despite the "cultural incongruence" of being mixed heritage or struggling to be an Indigenous woman surviving a residential school, the film demonstrates the long-standing resilience found out of the necessity of colonial dispossession.

CLEMENTINE BORDEAUX (Sicangu Oglala Lakota) is a doctoral student in culture and performance at the University of California, Los Angeles.

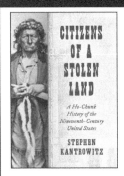

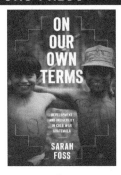

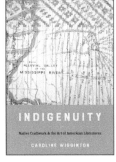

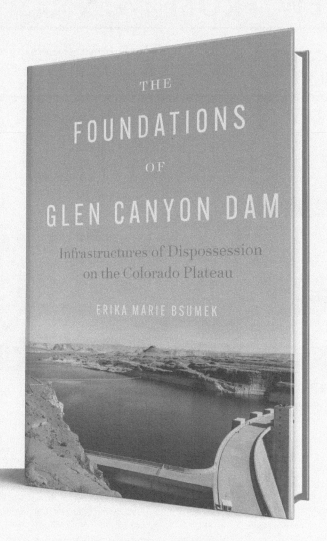

# NEW FROM MINNESOTA

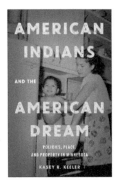

## American Indians and the American Dream
*Policies, Place, and Property in Minnesota*
Kasey R. Keeler

*American Indians and the American Dream* investigates the ways American Indians have accessed homeownership—working with and against federal policy—underscoring American Indian peoples' unequal and exclusionary access to the way of life known as the American dream.

$25.00 paperback | 256 pages | Available May 2023

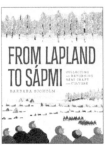

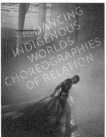

## From Lapland to Sápmi
*Collecting and Returning Sámi Craft and Culture*
Barbara Sjoholm

"An important contribution to Sámi stories of loss, recovery, and the struggle for equality, as well as the right to manage one's own cultural heritage on one's own terms." —**Káren Elle Gaup**, coeditor of *Bååstede: The Return of Sámi Cultural Heritage*

$34.95 hardcover | 368 pages | Available March 2023

## Natives against Nativism
*Antiracism and Indigenous Critique in Postcolonial France*
Olivia C. Harrison

"An invaluable work for scholars of race, coloniality, and indigeneity." —**Keith P. Feldman**, author of *A Shadow over Palestine: The Imperial Life of Race in America*

$28.00 paperback | 280 pages | Available April 2023

## Settling Nature
*The Conservation Regime in Palestine-Israel*
Irus Braverman

"[Examines] how the conservation of critical more-than-human natures sits at the heart of many of the most consequential and distressing power struggles of our time." —**Bram Büscher**, author of *The Truth about Nature: Environmentalism in the Era of Post-truth Politics and Platform Capitalism*

$29.00 paperback | 362 pages | Available April 2023

## Dancing Indigenous Worlds
*Choreographies of Relation*
Jacqueline Shea Murphy

"Confirms the intellectual possibilities of translating gesture to text and of moving with care." —**Thomas F. DeFrantz**, Northwestern University

$35.00 paperback | 408 pages

**University of Minnesota Press | www.upress.umn.edu | 800-621-2736**